Language Arts Tutor: Grammar, Capitalization, and Punctuation

Author: Cindy Barden
Editor: Mary Dieterich
Proofreaders: Lexi Albert and Margaret Brown

COPYRIGHT © 2017 Mark Twain Media, Inc.

ISBN 978-1-62223-632-9

Printing No. CD-404253

Mark Twain Media, Inc., Publishers
Distributed by Carson-Dellosa Publishing LLC

Visit us at www.carsondellosa.com

Table of Contents

Introduction

Students of all ability levels prefer interesting and readable material, particularly those who struggle with grammar, capitalization, and punctuation in their writing. This language arts activity book engages the interests of these students through individualized tutoring in highly readable, age-appropriate activities. It introduces and strengthens the concepts needed to build and reinforce grammar, capitalization, and punctuation skills for students in grades four through eight.

Designed in a lively, non-intimidating format, the reproducible activities include stories, exercises, games, riddles, and other stimulating materials to improve grammatical and language arts skills and enrich the learning experience for the struggling learner.

The activities in this book focus on learning to identify the basic parts of speech; matching nouns and pronouns in gender, case, and number; writing positive, comparative, and superlative adjectives and adverbs; and writing complete sentences with subjects and predicates that agree. Students will also learn capitalization and punctuation guidelines. Capitalization activities include working with names, places, quotations, and titles. Punctuation skills covered include commas, quotation marks, apostrophes, colons, semicolons, dashes, and end punctuation. The proper use of underlining and italics in titles is also discussed.

Definitions and examples on each page clearly explain the concept or skill reinforced by that activity. This format allows students to master one concept or skill at a time, thereby building confidence and proficiency.

Teachers, parents, and tutors can meet the special needs of students by selecting specific activities that reinforce the skills each student needs most.

Name: _Cory_ Date: _____

Nouns

A **noun** is a word that names a person, place, thing, or idea. *Egg, hiccup, flower, carpenter,* and *love* are nouns.

Directions: Underline the nouns in each sentence.

1. A regulation golf ball has 336 dimples.

2. Sharks are the only fish that can blink with both eyes.

3. In 1927, long-distance telephone service between New York and London cost $75.00 for the first three minutes.

4. Coin-operated pay telephones first appeared in 1899.

5. The yo-yo is not a recent invention: children in ancient Rome played with these toys made of wood or metal over 2,500 years ago.

Directions: For each category, write five nouns.

Plants	Transportation	Occupations
Pine Tree	Subway	Fisher
Tiger Lily	Plane	Lawyer
Rose	Car	doctor
Lavender	bike	artist
Acasia Tree	walking	voice actor

Weather Words	Places	Ideas
storm	London	Forever
rain	New York	Faith
Tornado	Japan	hope
Tsnami	China	Love
Sunny	Garden	eternal

Name: _____ Date: _____

Singular and Plural Nouns

Thurs

> **Nouns** can be singular or plural. **Singular** means one. **Plural** means more than one. Most nouns form their plurals by adding an *s* at the end of the word. *Pizzas, lawyers, noodles,* and *garages* are plural nouns.
>
> Words that end in *f, s, o,* and *y* are often exceptions to the rule. When in doubt, check a dictionary.
>
> **Antonyms** are words that mean the opposite. *Men* and *women; dogs* and *cats;* and *mountains* and *valleys* are antonyms.

Directions: Write the plurals. Use a dictionary to check the spelling.

1. leaf _____
2. fly _____
3. trophy _____
4. elf _____
5. hippopotamus _____
6. sky _____
7. bus _____
8. ox _____
9. address _____
10. box _____

Directions: For each noun, write another noun that is an antonym.

11. questions _____
12. adults _____
13. friends _____
14. days _____
15. ceilings _____
16. slavery _____
17. smile _____

Name: _____ Date: _____

Irregular Noun Plurals

The **spellings** of some nouns change completely from singular to plural, as in *child - children; mouse - mice.*

Both the singular and plural of some nouns are spelled the same, for example: *deer - deer.*

Directions: Write the plurals of these nouns. Use a dictionary if you need help.

Singular	**Plural**
1. man	_____
2. woman	_____
3. goose	_____
4. louse	_____
5. scissors	_____
6. sheep	_____
7. moose	_____
8. tooth	_____
9. foot	_____
10. fish	_____
11. cattle	_____
12. data	_____
13. crisis	_____
14. bacterium	_____
15. analysis	_____
16. pants	_____
17. fungus	_____
18. index	_____
19. focus	_____
20. appendix	_____

Name: _____ Date: _____

Proper Nouns

> A **proper noun** is a noun that names a specific person, place, or thing. *Harry Potter, Mississippi River, Mount Vesuvius,* and *London Bridge* are proper nouns.

Directions: Underline the proper nouns in the following sentences.

1. The 60-foot-high heads of four presidents, George Washington, Thomas Jefferson, Abraham Lincoln, and Theodore Roosevelt, were carved on Mount Rushmore in the Black Hills of South Dakota by Gutzon Borglum.

2. Yellowstone National Park in Wyoming, Montana, and Idaho became the first national park in 1872 by order of President Ulysses S. Grant.

3. Eight states, Maine, Maryland, Massachusetts, Michigan, Minnesota, Mississippi, Missouri, and Montana, begin with *m*.

4. Harriet Tubman, known as the "Moses of her people," led slaves to freedom on the Underground Railroad.

5. We celebrate Thanksgiving on the fourth Thursday in November.

Directions: Use the Internet or other reference sources to find one interesting fact about each topic. Write a sentence about each topic that includes at least four proper nouns.

6. An athlete: _____

_____

7. A city, state, or country: _____

_____

8. A lake, river, or ocean: _____

_____

9. A book, movie, or play: _____

_____

Name: _____ Date: _____

Action Verbs

A **verb** is a word that shows action or being. *Tiptoe, bounce,* and *fly* are action verbs.

Directions: Write an action verb that begins with each letter of the alphabet. For *x*, use any verb that contains the letter *x*.

A _____

B _____

C _____

D _____

E _____

F _____

G _____

H _____

I _____

J _____

K _____

L _____

M _____

N _____

O _____

P _____

Q _____

R _____

S _____

T _____

U _____

V _____

W _____

X _____

Y _____

Z _____

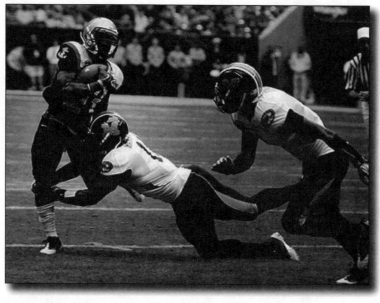

Name: _____ Date: _____

Singular and Plural Verbs

Nouns that end in an *s* are usually **plural**. Some examples are: *The boys go; The girls sing; The birds chirp.* **Verbs** that end in *s* are usually **singular**. Some examples are: *She goes; He sings; It chirps.*

Directions: Write the missing form of each verb.

	Singular	Plural
1.	plays	_____
2.	_____	guess
3.	_____	cough
4.	wishes	_____
5.	growls	_____
6.	_____	drive
7.	displays	_____
8.	thinks	_____
9.	_____	wax
10.	_____	dance

Directions: Write *S* for singular or *P* for plural on the blanks. Underline the verbs.

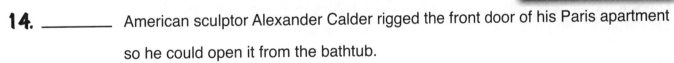

11. _____ People with phobatrivaphobia fear trivia about phobias.

12. _____ No matter how hard you try, you cannot lick your elbow.

13. _____ Male lions sleep up to 20 hours per day.

14. _____ American sculptor Alexander Calder rigged the front door of his Paris apartment

so he could open it from the bathtub.

15. _____ A cockroach runs one meter per second.

16. _____ For a short distance, a hippopotamus can run faster than a person.

17. _____ Many students suffer from didaskaleinophobia.

18. _____ Didaskaleinophobia means the fear of going to school.

Verbs of Being

A **verb** is a word that shows action or being. Verbs of being include *feel, look, sound, taste, appear, grow, seem, smell,* and forms of *be.* Forms of *be* include *am, are, is, was, were, be,* and *been.*

Verbs of being are usually followed by a noun(s) or adjective(s) that shows a relationship.

Glenda is <u>happy</u>. (Adjective)   *Glen was <u>lonely</u> and <u>scared</u>.* (Adjectives)

Gwendolyn is a <u>girl</u>. (Noun)   *Is your favorite pattern <u>plaid</u> or <u>polka-dots</u>?* (Nouns)

Directions: Circle the verbs of being. Underline the two words that show a relationship. The first one has been done as an example.

1. <u>Pizza</u> ⬭tastes⬭ <u>great</u>.

2. Frankenstein felt hungry after he awoke.

3. He said, "Dinner smells delicious."

4. Did Spencer appear sad when you saw him after the movie?

5. A zebra is white with black stripes.

6. Did Grandpa feel sleepy after dinner?

7. They were elated at the good news.

8. My sister grew four inches taller last year.

9. You seem worried about something.

10. Hippopotomonstrosesquippedaliophobia is the fear of long words.

Directions: Write two sentences that use verbs of being about your favorite short story. Then circle the verbs of being and underline the two words that show a relationship.

_____

_____

_____

_____

_____

Name: _____ Date: _____

Verb Tense

Verbs use tense to show the time of the action.

- **Present tense** describes what is happening now.

    He *is using* *his new computer.*   *He* *uses* *his computer daily.*

- **Past tense** describes what has already happened.

    She *bought* *a new computer program last week.*

- **Future tense** describes what will happen.

    We *will buy* *a new computer in July.*

Directions: Circle the verbs. Write *PR* for present, *PA* for past, or *F* for future.

1. _____ Joel washed his St. Bernard in the bathtub.

2. _____ Joel named his dog Minnie.

3. _____ Joel takes Minnie to obedience school every Tuesday.

4. _____ Minnie will learn to fetch large objects.

5. _____ Joel loves Minnie.

6. _____ The bears at the Cincinnati Zoo hibernated

last winter.

7. _____ Did the bears at the San Diego Zoo hibernate?

8. _____ Will the groundhog see its shadow on February second?

9. _____ Can you come to the cottage next weekend?

10. _____ No one came to Sara's party last Saturday.

Directions: Write a verb in the tense indicated to finish the sentence.

11. Future tense: One of the major league teams _____ Geoff.

12. Past tense: Who _____ first base for the Brewers last year?

13. Present tense: Tina _____ five miles every day.

Name: _____ Date: _____

Three Forms of Verbs

Verbs have three main forms: **present**, **past**, and **past participle**.

Use *had* with the past tense of a verb to form the **past perfect tense** of the **past participle** of regular verbs. Ad *-d* or *-ed* to form the **past tense** of most verbs.

They <u>had played</u> all day at the beach.   *She <u>walked</u> on the trail yesterday.*

For one-syllable words ending in a single consonant preceded by a vowel, double the final consonant before adding *-ed*. For words ending in *y* after a consonant, change the *y* to *i* and add *-ed*.

For example:

Present	Past	Past Participle
hug	*hugged*	*had hugged*
skip	*skipped*	*had skipped*
party	*partied*	*had partied*

Directions: Write the missing verb forms for these regular verbs. Use a dictionary if you need help.

Present	Past	Past Participle
1. sail	_____	_____
2. mop	_____	_____
3. empty	_____	_____
4. jump	_____	_____
5. try	_____	_____
6. believe	_____	_____
7. sip	_____	_____
8. fry	_____	_____
9. push	_____	_____
10. imply	_____	_____
11. mope	_____	_____
12. plant	_____	_____

Name: _____ Date: _____

Irregular Verbs

The **past** and **past participle** forms of most verbs are formed by adding *-d* or *-ed*. Verbs that do not follow this rule are called **irregular verbs**.

Present	Past	Past Participle
bring	brought	had brought
buy	bought	had bought
go	went	had gone
do	did	had done
fly	flew	had flown
grow	grew	had grown
ride	rode	had ridden
see	saw	had seen
sing	sang	had sung
swim	swam	had swum
throw	threw	had thrown

Do not use the past tense form of an irregular verb with the word *had*.

Correct: He <u>had flown</u> the plane to Florida.
Incorrect: He <u>had flew</u> the plane to Florida.

The word *had* can be separated from the verb by other words in the sentence.
<u>Had</u> you <u>seen</u> my blue sweater?

Directions: Using the irregular verb chart above, complete the sentences by writing the correct form of the verb shown in parentheses.

1. Had you ever _____ a camel? (ride)

2. Coach replaced the quarterback because he had _____ too many interceptions. (throw)

3. I can't believe he _____ that pass! (catch)

4. Her fig tree had _____ three inches taller while she was on vacation. (grow)

5. Where do you _____ when you want peace and quiet? (go)

6. Jerrod _____ to Phoenix for the winter. (go)

7. Had you ever _____ a sight like that? (see)

8. Cal _____ a jar of peanuts at the store. (buy)

Name: _____ Date: _____

Complete Sentences

A **sentence** is a group of words that expresses a complete thought.

The White House did not have indoor plumbing until 1902.

- An incomplete sentence is called a **fragment**.

The Blue Room at the White House where the first lady.

- Every sentence needs a **subject** and a **predicate**. The **subject** is the person or thing that does something. The **predicate** is the action that is done or a description of the state of being of the subject. In some sentences, the subject is *you*, and it is understood but not stated.

Please close the door.   *Help!*

- A **simple sentence** has one subject and one predicate. A **compound sentence** has two or more subjects and/or predicates.

Directions: Read each group of words. If it expresses a complete thought, write *yes* on the blank. If not, write *no*.

1. George Washington never lived in the White House. _____

2. A contest for the best design. _____

3. A fire in 1814 during the War of 1812. _____

4. During renovations to the White House between 1938 and 1952, the number of rooms increased

from 62 to 132. _____

5. In spite of the many changes that have taken place, the White House and home of the President

and his family. _____

6. Write a sentence with two subjects and one predicate.

_____

_____

7. Write a sentence with one subject and two predicates.

_____

_____

Name: _____   Date: _____

Kinds of Sentences

Capitalize the first word of a sentence. All sentences end with a period, question mark, or exclamation point.

- A sentence that states a fact or gives a command ends in a **period**.

  The walrus frowned at the iceberg.   *Please hand me that pencil.*

- A sentence that asks a question ends with a **question mark**.

  Would you hand me that pencil?   *Where is the walrus now?*

- A sentence that shows strong emotion ends with an **exclamation point**.

  That's a great idea!   *Look out!*

Directions: Write a complete sentence that shows strong emotion for each situation.

1. You won a terrific prize in the contest.

_____

2. Todd found his missing pet snake.

_____

Directions: Write three sentences that are commands but not questions.

3. _____

4. _____

5. _____

Directions: For each answer, write a short question.

6. _____ hot dogs

7. _____ bats

8. _____ 10 points

Directions: Add punctuation at the end of each sentence.

9. Why did the turkey cross the road

10. It was the chicken's day off

11. That's hilarious

12. Tell me another one, please

Name: _____ Date: _____

Simple Predicates

The **simple predicate** of a sentence tells what the subject does, is doing, did, or will do. The simple predicate is always a **verb**.

The cat <u>sneezed</u>. (physical action)   *Josh <u>thought</u> about the joke.* (mental action)

Althea <u>is</u> sick. (state of being)

A sentence may have two or more predicates.

Althea <u>coughed</u>, <u>sneezed</u>, and <u>blew</u> her nose.

Directions: Circle the simple predicates. Write *A* if the verb is active, or *B* if the verb describes a state of being.

1. _____ The hungry dog ate the violin.

2. _____ Carlos danced in the forest.

3. _____ Would you please pass the sour milk?

4. _____ Eight green-eyed aliens arrived yesterday.

5. _____ Mustard is better with hot dogs than peanut butter or jelly.

6. _____ Tina baked and ate a jelly-bean pizza.

7. _____ Jake traveled by submarine, and Angie rode in a hot-air balloon from California to New York.

8. _____ We are thrilled about our latest invention of breathable water.

9. _____ Macaroni is not a good material for building a house.

10. _____ Glass houses have brick fireplaces, but brick houses do not have glass fireplaces.

Directions: Write simple predicates to finish the sentences.

11. Felipe _____ the hot chili peppers.

12. I _____, he _____, and she _____ when we watched the strange movie.

Name: _____ Date: _____

Simple Subjects

> The **simple subject** of a sentence is a noun or pronoun that is doing something or being something.
>
> Subjects can be singular or plural.
>
> _Miss Muffet_ and three _spiders_ ate lunch together.
>
> More than one noun or pronoun can be the subject of a sentence.
>
> _Mary's little lamb, Bo Peep's sheep, and my little red hen_ searched for the treasure.

Directions: Circle the simple subjects. Remember, only nouns or pronouns can be the subjects, but not all nouns or pronouns in a sentence *are* subjects.

1. The big, bad wolf blew down the house made of sticks.

2. Can you and Little Boy Blue help Bo Peep find her sheep?

3. Jack jumped over the candlestick.

4. Can a cow jump over the moon?

5. The dish ran away with the spoon.

6. Did the mouse run up the clock?

7. Jack and Jill ran up the hill.

8. How do oats, peas, beans, and barley grow?

9. Jack jumped over the candlestick, and Mary chased her little lamb.

10. Old King Cole, his three fiddlers, the Knave of Hearts, and three blind mice went to the fair.

Directions: Write nouns or pronouns in the blanks to finish the sentences.

11. _____, _____, and _____ rode the rhinoceros.

12. _____ found a penny, and _____ picked it up.

13. _____ and _____ danced around the mulberry bush.

14. What did _____ find at the end of the rainbow?

Name: _____   Date: _____

Agreement of Subjects and Predicates

The subjects and predicates of a sentence **must agree in number**. If the subject is singular, then the predicate is singular.

Marnie sings like a canary.   *She is a good singer.*

If the subject is plural, then the predicate is plural. Use a plural verb in a sentence that has two or more singular subjects.

Daniel and Danielle sing well together.   *They are twins.*

Directions: Underline the subjects. Write *S* for singular or *P* for plural. Then write active verbs to finish the sentences.

1. _____ Lizards and snakes _____ in Florida.

2. _____ Everyone _____ bagpipe music.

3. _____ Chili with hot peppers _____ great.

4. _____ A squirrel, a snail, and a skunk _____ to the picnic.

5. _____ If a pig could _____, we would cheer.

6. _____ Does money _____ on trees on Venus?

7. _____ Does anyone still _____ that the earth is flat?

8. _____ The village _____ deep in the forest.

Directions: Write *S* for singular or *P* for plural to describe the verb. Then write nouns to finish the sentences.

9. _____ _____ fly.

10. _____ _____ dances.

11. _____ _____ bakes pumpkin bread.

12. _____ _____ eat sunflower seeds.

13. _____ _____ goes to the moon.

14. _____ _____ is tired.

15. _____ _____ march down the road.

Name: _____ Date: _____

Pronouns as Subjects

Pronouns take the place of nouns. They refer to people, places, things, or ideas.

The **antecedent** is the word replaced by a pronoun. If the antecedent is singular, use a singular pronoun. If the antecedent is plural, use a plural pronoun to replace it.

These pronouns can be used as subjects of sentences:

Singular	**Plural**
I	we
you	you
she, he, it	they

Directions: Write pronouns to replace the words in parentheses.

1. (The dragon) _____ breathed fire.

2. (The knight) _____ threw a bucket of water.

3. (The dragon) _____ began to steam.

4. (The men and women) _____ shouted, "Hurray!"

5. (The girl) _____ watched the knight ride his black horse into the sunset.

6. (Jamie and I) _____ want to be knights someday.

Directions: Write nouns to replace the underlined pronouns.

7. <u>We</u> _____ made friends with aliens from a distant galaxy.

8. <u>They</u> _____ traveled to Earth through time and space in a unique spaceship.

9. <u>It</u> _____ used carrot juice for fuel.

10. <u>He</u> _____ invited the aliens to visit the White House.

11. <u>She</u> _____ prepared 10,000 gallons of fresh carrot juice.

12. When the ship was refueled, <u>they</u> _____ took us to their planet.

Possessive Pronouns

Possessive pronouns show ownership.

Possessive pronouns are:

	Singular	**Plural**
	my, mine	*our, ours*
	your, yours	*your, yours*
	her, hers, his, its	*their, theirs*

Possessive pronouns must agree with their antecedents in **number** (singular or plural) and **gender** (male, female, or neuter).

The dog went into its house.   *The children lost their way in the forest.*

Directions: Fill in the blanks with possessive pronouns.

1. Marcy's trumpet is _____ trumpet. That trumpet is _____.

2. The tuba I play in the band is _____ tuba. That tuba is _____.

3. Jamal's bass drum is _____ drum. That bass drum is _____.

4. A treasure that belongs to you and me is _____ treasure.

   That treasure is _____.

5. Ted and Mei's song is _____ song. That song is _____.

6. The story you wrote last week is _____ story. That story is _____.

7. A hippo's loose tooth is _____ tooth.

8. The home where you and your family live is _____ home.

   That home is _____.

9. The horse's tail is _____ tail.

10. The brush I use is _____ brush. That brush is _____.

11. Sarah's dog is _____ dog. That dog is _____.

12. Mom and Dad's car is _____ car. That car is _____.

13. The book that belongs to Jackson is _____ book. That book is _____.

14. The food you and I eat is _____ food. That food is _____.

Name: _____   Date: _____

Contractions and Possessive Pronouns

Contractions are two words combined. An apostrophe shows that letters are missing.

Some contractions are often confused with possessive pronouns.

Contractions

you're = you are   *it's = it is*
they're = they are   *there's = there is*

Possessive Pronouns

your = belonging to you   *its = belonging to it*
their = belonging to them   *theirs = belonging to them*

Directions: Circle the correct words.

1. "(You're, Your) late," our coach complained.

2. "Put on (you're, your) uniform quickly," he continued.

3. "The rest of the team already put on (there's, theirs)."

4. "(There's, Theirs) no time to waste."

5. "(It's, Its) (you're, your) turn to bring the equipment."

6. "(They're, Their) ready to begin."

7. "The horseshoes are in (they're, their) cases."

8. "The stopwatch is in (it's, its) case on my desk."

Directions: Write a sentence using the pronoun or contraction listed.

9. they're _____

_____

10. its _____

_____

11. your _____

_____

12. theirs _____

_____

Name: _____ Date: _____

Direct and Indirect Objects

A **direct object** is a noun or pronoun. It answers the question *who* or *what* after the verb.

Mom bakes <u>bread</u>.   *Bread* is the direct object. It tells *what* Mom baked.

Mr. Clark hired <u>Randy</u> and <u>Lynn</u> to rake leaves.   *Randy* and *Lynn* are both direct objects. They tell *who* Mr. Clark hired.

An **indirect object** is a noun or pronoun. It answers the question *to whom* or *for whom* the action is performed. An indirect object is usually found between a verb and a direct object.

I gave <u>Elias</u> my e-mail address.   *Elias* is the indirect object. It tells *to whom* I gave my e-mail address.

Directions: Underline the direct objects.

1. Carla brought pizza, cake, and ice cream for the party.

2. Benji decorated the room and hung streamers in the windows.

3. Randy and Lynn raked leaves for Mr. Clark.

4. After Tasha sang the last song, the audience threw flowers.

5. Did Mia ride her bike or her motorcycle to school today?

Directions: Circle the indirect objects. Underline the direct objects.

6. Who gave Pedro that awful haircut?

7. Ellen sent Todd and Tami a wedding gift.

8. Mr. Clark gave Randy and Lynn $20.00 for their work.

9. Grandpa told Andy and Tori a story.

10. Uncle Joel showed Heather a magic trick.

11. Kimiko sang the baby a lullaby.

12. Did you give Devin the book?

Name: _____ Date: _____

Interrogative Pronouns

Who, what, and *which* are **interrogative pronouns**.

Use *who* when speaking of a person or persons.

> <u>Who</u> wore the cowboy hat?   The man <u>who</u> wore the cowboy hat was tall.

Use *what* when speaking of things.

> <u>What</u> fell from the sky?   No one knew <u>what</u> had fallen from the sky.

Use *which* when speaking of persons or things.

> <u>Which</u> woman wore the white woolen gown?
> <u>Which</u> do you like better: jugglers or clowns?

Who changes to *whom* when it is a direct object or an object of a preposition.

> To <u>whom</u> did you send the e-mail?

The possessive form of *whom* is *whose*.

> <u>Whose</u> e-mail address did you use?

Directions: Write *who, whom, whose, which,* or *what* in the blanks.

1. _____ movie won the most awards?

2. _____ played the leading role?

3. _____ fault was it that no one arrived on time?

4. Ask not for _____ the bell tolls.

5. The scientists found the answer for _____ they had been searching.

6. To _____ do we owe the honor of your presence?

7. _____ idea do you like best: Maria's or Joel's?

8. To _____ should we send the money order?

Name: _____ Date: _____

Adjectives

An **adjective** is a word that describes a noun or pronoun. *Smelly, silly,* and *short* are adjectives.

Separate three or more adjectives in a row with a comma whether or not the word *and* is used.

Marty put the <u>large, frozen, mushroom</u> pizza in the oven.

Brett had three slices of the <u>hot, fresh, and delicious</u> homemade bread.

Directions: Write three or more adjectives to describe each noun. The first one has been done as an example.

1. _*stinky, crumbly, Limburger*_____ cheese

2. _____ music

3. _____ software

4. _____ park

5. _____ library

6. _____ texture

7. _____ pineapple

8. _____ judge

9. _____ carpet

10. _____ weather

11. _____ jungle

12. _____ movie

13. _____ video game

14. _____ mountain

15. _____ cloud

Name: _____   Date: _____

Comparative and Superlative Adjectives

Adjectives have three forms: **positive, comparative,** and **superlative**.

- The **positive** form is the adjective itself.

  Rosa thinks daisies are <u>pretty</u>.

- Use the **comparative** form to compare two people, places, things, or ideas.

  Rosa thinks daisies are <u>prettier</u> than violets.

- Use the **superlative** form when comparing three or more items.

  Daisy thinks roses are the <u>prettiest</u> flowers of all.

Guidelines:

Add -*er* at the end of most one-syllable adjectives to form the **comparative**.
For two-syllable words ending in *y*, change the *y* to *i* and add -*er*. *(happier)*
For short words ending in *e*, simply add *r*. *(wider)*
For short words with the consonant/vowel/consonant (CVC) pattern, double the final consonant before adding -*er*. *(hotter)*
When in doubt, check a dictionary.

Directions: Write the comparative or superlative form of an adjective in each sentence.

1. Is Flora _____ than Violet?

2. What is the _____ mountain on Mars?

3. Which river is _____, the Amazon or the Nile?

4. Where is the _____ canyon in North America?

5. Have you ever seen falls _____ than Niagara Falls?

6. The _____ day on record was at the South Pole.

7. It rarely gets _____ than 85 degrees in Hawaii.

8. For each pair, the winner is the one who runs _____.

9. The tortoise was _____ than the hare, but he won the race.

10. Of all mammals, which runs the _____?

11. Is it _____ to dribble a basketball or throw a football?

12. Jaden has the _____ job on the team.

Name: _____ Date: _____

Comparative and Superlative Forms of Longer Adjectives

Combine the adjective with the word *more/less* or *most/least* to form the **comparative** and **superlative** form of most two-syllable words that do not end in *y*.

Form the comparative and superlative form of all adjectives with three or more syllables by combining the adjective with the word *more/less* or *most/least*.

Positive	Comparative	Superlative
modern	*less modern*	*least modern*
beautiful	*more beautiful*	*most beautiful*

Some adjectives change completely to form the comparative and superlative, such as *good – better – best*.

Directions: Write the comparative and superlative forms of these adjectives.

Positive	Comparative	Superlative
1. floppy	_____	_____
2. slow	_____	_____
3. expensive	_____	_____
4. happy	_____	_____
5. late	_____	_____
6. heavy	_____	_____

Directions: Write the comparative and superlative forms of these adjectives. Use a dictionary if you need help.

Positive	Comparative	Superlative
7. far	_____	_____
8. bad	_____	_____
9. many	_____	_____
10. well (healthy)	_____	_____
11. ill	_____	_____
12. little (amount)	_____	_____

Name: _____ Date: _____

Adverbs

An **adverb** is a word that modifies a verb, adjective, or another adverb by describing, limiting, or making the meaning of a word more clear.

Eric Carle wrote *The Very Hungry Caterpillar.*

The word *very* is an adverb that modifies the adjective *hungry*. It tells *how* hungry.

Adverbs answer the questions *why, where, when, how,* or *to what extent.*

Tomorrow, far, shortly, quickly, and *abruptly* are adverbs.

Directions: Circle the adverb(s) in each sentence. Underline the word(s) it modifies. Write the question the adverb answers. The first one has been done as an example.

1. The truck driver <u>unloaded</u> the trailer (quickly.)

   How did the driver unload the trailer?

2. She drove eagerly to the next truck stop.

_____

3. After a short rest, she filled the gas tank completely.

_____

4. She traveled far on the long, winding mountain road.

_____

5. She will arrive in Denver tomorrow.

_____

6. She played the radio quietly while she drove.

_____

7. Too soon, it began to snow.

_____

8. The snow-covered road eventually became very slippery.

_____

_____

Name: _____   Date: _____

Comparative and Superlative Adverbs

Like adjectives, **adverbs** have three forms: **positive, comparative,** and **superlative**.

- The **positive** form is the adverb itself.

  Jason will be here <u>soon</u>.

- Use the **comparative** form to compare two events.

  Jason will arrive <u>sooner</u> than Grandpa.

- Use the **superlative** form when comparing three or more items.

  Of all the guests, Jason will arrive the <u>soonest</u>.

Guidelines:

- Add *-er* to the end of most one-syllable adverbs to form the **comparative**.
- Add *-est* to the end of most one-syllable adverbs to form the **superlative**.
- For most adverbs ending in *-ly,* combine the adverb with the word *more* or *less* for **comparative**, and *most* or *least* for **superlative**.

brightly	*more brightly*	*most brightly*
noisily	*less noisily*	*least noisily*

Some adverbs are irregular. When in doubt, check a dictionary.

Directions: Write the comparative or superlative form of an adjective in each sentence.

1. Is Chantal reading _____ than she did yesterday?

2. She acted the _____ of all the students.

3. Ask the children to play _____ than they did yesterday.

4. Dion takes life much _____ than his sister does.

5. This book is written _____ than the last one by the same author.

6. He unwrapped the second package _____ than he did the first one.

7. Mike did badly on the test, but Jeremy did even _____.

8. Which of the three statues do you think is _____ carved?

9. This bus will get you to the mall _____ than the next one.

10. Of all the dancers, she twirls the _____.

Name: _____   Date: _____

Adjective or Adverb?

Many **adjectives** can be changed to an adverb by adding *-ly* to the end of the word. If the word ends in *y*, change the *y* to *i*, and add *-ly*.

quiet	quietly	slow	slowly
hungry	hungrily	dainty	daintily

Use an **adjective** to describe a noun or pronoun. Use an **adverb** to modify a verb, adjective, or other adverb.

He made a *quick* trip to the store.   *Quick* is an adjective describing *trip*.

He ran *quickly* to the store.   *Quickly* is an adverb. It tells how he ran.

Directions: State whether the underlined word in each sentence is an adjective (ADJ) or an adverb (ADV) and why.

1. He has <u>strong</u> feelings for his brother. _____

Why? _____

2. He felt <u>strongly</u> that his brother was wrong. _____

Why? _____

3. I can tell when danger is <u>near</u>. _____

Why? _____

4. Are we <u>nearly</u> there? _____

Why? _____

5. Take me to the <u>nearest</u> ice cream stand. _____

Why? _____

6. The trail is <u>longer</u> than I thought it would be. _____

Why? _____

7. Joanne giggled <u>happily</u>. _____

Why? _____

8. Tony's dog won <u>first</u> prize. _____

Why? _____

9. Which came <u>first</u>: the chicken or the egg? _____

Why? _____

10. Tomorrow is <u>another</u> day. _____

Why? _____

Name: _____   Date: _____

Prepositions and Prepositional Phrases

A **preposition** is a word that comes before a noun or pronoun and shows its relationship to some other word in the sentence.

Common Prepositions

about	down	off	through	above	for	on	to
across	from	out	up	at	in	over	with
behind	into	near	within	by	of	past	without

The **object of a preposition** is a noun or pronoun that follows a preposition and adds to its meaning. A preposition must be followed by a noun or pronoun.

A **prepositional phrase** includes the preposition, the object of the preposition, and all modifiers.

Gertrude Ederle was the first woman to swim across the English Channel.

Across is the preposition.
Across the English Channel is the prepositional phrase.
English Channel is the object of the preposition.

Directions: Complete the prepositional phrases. Underline the prepositions. Circle the nouns or pronouns that are objects of the prepositions.

1. _____ the flea circus

2. _____ the tallest tree

3. inside the empty _____

4. without any possible _____

5. past the _____ mountains

6. _____ the ice-covered rooftops

7. _____ the dark and gloomy forest

8. near the _____ ancient castle

9. _____ the south side of the _____

10. _____ the _____

Name: _____   Date: _____

Identifying Prepositions and Prepositional Phrases

A **preposition** is a word that comes before a noun or pronoun and shows its relationship to some other word in the sentence.

A **proverb** is a saying that most people accept as true and that implies a deeper meaning.

"When in Rome, do as the Romans do."

Directions: Underline the prepositions and enclose the prepositional phrases in parentheses. Circle the nouns or pronouns that are the objects of the prepositions. The first one has been done as an example. Some proverbs may contain more than one prepositional phrase.

1. Don't cry (<u>over</u> spilt (milk)).

2. A bird in the hand is worth two in the bush.

3. A journey of a thousand miles begins with a single step.

4. People in glass houses should not throw stones.

5. Never look a gift horse in the mouth.

6. The grass is always greener on the other side of the fence.

7. Rome wasn't built in a day.

8. Birds of a feather flock together.

9. Necessity is the mother of invention.

10. Great oaks from little acorns grow.

11. You can't make a silk purse from a sow's ear.

12. It's all water under the bridge.

Directions: Select one of the above proverbs and rewrite it in your own words. "Don't cry over spilt milk" could be rewritten as: "If you can't do something about a situation, move on."

_____

_____

_____

Name: _____ Date: _____

Objective Pronouns

Use **objective pronouns** as direct objects, indirect objects, or objects of a preposition.

Objective Pronouns

Singular: *me, you, him, her, it*   **Plural:** *us, you, them*

Two or more nouns or pronouns can be the direct objects of a sentence.

> *Aunt June met <u>him</u> and <u>me</u> at the bus station.*

> *Dana liked <u>him</u> better than <u>her</u>.*

Two or more nouns or pronouns can be the objects of a preposition.

> *Dave played the game with <u>her</u> and <u>him</u>.*

> *Mom received gifts from <u>her</u> and <u>me</u>.*

Directions: Fill in the blanks with objective pronouns. Write *DO* for direct object, *IO* for indirect object, or *OP* for object of a preposition within the parentheses to show how each pronoun is used.

1. Tina saw _____ and _____ at the pool. (_____)

2. Will you meet _____ at Pier 49? (_____)

3. The party was for _____ and _____. (_____)

4. The plumber gave _____ and _____ the bad news. (_____)

5. Marsha received phone calls from _____ and _____. (_____)

6. Mom gave _____ a pail, and Dad gave _____ a broom. (_____)

7. Tiffany lent the book to _____, but Dave forgot to give it back to _____.

   (_____)

8. Uncle Frank brought _____ and _____ souvenirs from the North Pole.

   (_____)

9. Did Buster drive _____ and _____ to San Francisco? (_____)

10. Are you going to the amusement park with _____? (_____)

Name: _____ Date: _____

Homophones

Homophones are words that sound the same but are spelled differently and have different meanings.

He knew the new gnu would be at the zoo today.

Directions: Circle the correct word in each pair. Write the part of speech of the word you circled on the line next to the sentence. Use a dictionary if you need help.

1. _____ Our ship (sails, sales) for
   _____ Cancun next (weak, week).

2. _____ I can't (wait, weight)
   _____ (to, two, too) leave.

3. _____ Jean bought her jeans on (sail, sale).

4. _____ She paid full price for the first (pair, pear)
   _____ and only 99 (sense, cents) for the second one.

5. _____ Do you like (red, read) roses
   _____ or (blew, blue) carnations better?

6. _____ When the (brakes, breaks) failed, his car slid down the hill.

7. _____ Clark lost his (way, weigh)
   _____ when he (maid, made) a
   _____ (write, right) turn in a small town
   _____ in (Maine, Main).

8. _____ Don't (stair, stare) at the man
   _____ wearing the (fur, fir) shirt.

9. _____ Sandy looked (pail, pale)
   _____ because she had the (flu, flew).

10. _____ He (knew, new) that
   _____ (four, for, fore) plus
   _____ (to, two, too) equals
   _____ six, but he didn't (no, know)
   _____ that seven plus (won, one)
   _____ equals (ate, eight)?

Name: _____   Date: _____

Conjunctions

> **Conjunctions** are words that connect two or more words or groups of words. *And, but, or, nor, so,* and *because* are conjunctions.
>
> Join two short sentences with the word *and* when the sentences are about equal.
>
> > *Juan will arrive at noon, <u>and</u> he will be hungry.*
>
> Join two short sentences with the word *but* when the second sentence contradicts the first.
>
> > *Juan will arrive at lunchtime, <u>but</u> he will not be hungry.*
>
> Join two short sentences with the word *or* when they name a choice.
>
> > *Juan may be on time, <u>or</u> he may be late.*
>
> Join two short sentences with *because* or *so* when the second sentence names a reason for the first sentence.
>
> > *Juan will be on time <u>because</u> he is very punctual.*

Directions: Write conjunctions to complete the sentences.

1. Barry doesn't like prune juice, _____ he likes prunes.

2. Tori overslept, _____ she was late for school.

3. Would you like ham on your pizza, _____ would you

rather have tuna?

4. The river overflowed _____ the dam broke.

5. I could go to the movie, _____ I could go to Sarah's party.

6. Reggie didn't know where the popcorn was _____ we had chips instead.

7. My favorite color is purple, _____ irises are my favorite flower.

Directions: Finish the sentences.

8. Marta will sing in the choir, or _____

9. Marta will sing in the choir because _____

10. Marta will sing in the choir, and _____

Name: _____ Date: _____

More Than One Part of Speech

Some words can be used **as more than one part of speech.**

Dance can be a noun, a verb, or an adjective.

> *Would you like to go to the <u>dance</u>?* (noun)
>
> *Will you <u>dance</u> with me tomorrow?* (verb)
>
> *The <u>dance</u> instructor taught me to waltz.* (adjective)

Directions: Write short sentences using the words as the parts of speech indicated in parentheses. Use a dictionary if you need help. Use your own paper if you need more room.

1. dress (noun) _____

    dress (verb) _____

    dress (adjective) _____

2. guard (noun) _____

    guard (verb) _____

    guard (adjective) _____

3. light (noun) _____

    light (verb) _____

    light (adjective) _____

4. brown (noun) _____

    brown (verb) _____

    brown (adjective) _____

5. mine (pronoun) _____

    mine (noun) _____

    mine (verb) _____

Parts of Speech Bingo Card

Directions to the Teacher: Give each student a copy of a blank Parts of Speech Bingo card and game markers (buttons, slips of paper, dry beans, or kernels of corn can be used). Have students write the name of one of these parts of speech in each square: noun, pronoun, adjective, adverb, verb, or preposition.

Make a copy of the word list on the next two pages on heavy paper or light cardboard. Cut the words apart and place them in a bag. Draw one word at a time. Read the word to the class, using it in a sentence, and then write the part of speech on the slip of paper with the word. Students should cover the square on their Bingo card that matches that part of speech. Play like regular Bingo. Have students write the word in the square, so you can check if the correct part of speech has been chosen.

		Free		

Parts of Speech Bingo Word List

about	briskly	dizzy	fluffy	grandly	in
air	broken	down	flutes	greedy	instant
alertly	bumpy	drably	foggy	grimy	it
almost	bus	drowsy	fondly	grumpy	itchy
always	butter	drums	forest	gusty	its
among	cake	dusty	forever	hairy	jolly
around	calmly	eager	former	happily	joy
at	candy	eagerly	forward	happy	judge
ate	carry	early	fragile	hastily	juicy
badly	cattle	easily	frantic	he	jump
banker	city	elegant	freely	healthy	jumpy
barely	cleanly	empty	fresh	hear	jungle
barn	clearly	entire	freshly	heavily	kind
beans	closely	equal	frisky	heavy	kindly
beauty	coat	equally	from	helpful	largely
before	coldly	eternal	frosty	hers	largest
behind	coolly	evenly	frozen	hidden	lately
between	country	exact	fully	highly	lazily
big	crisply	exactly	funny	hilly	leafy
bitter	daily	exotic	furry	him	level
black	darkly	extreme	fuzzy	his	lightly
bleak	day	famous	gentle	hog	little
boat	dearly	fancy	gently	honest	lizard
bond	deeply	farmer	give	honesty	lonely
bored	desert	fearful	gladly	hop	loudly
brave	dimly	feel	glassy	humid	love
bravely	dimples	final	gloomy	I	lovely
breezy	direct	flatly	goat	ideal	luckily
bright	dirty	fleet	golden	ideally	lucky
brisk	distant	flower	grand	ideas	lumpy

Parts of Speech Bingo Word List (cont.)

mainly	once	rainy	skip	total	whisker
marshy	our	rake	sleep	toward	widely
mellow	ours	rapid	slowly	toy	willing
mildly	over	rapidly	smell	truly	wince
mine	oxen	rarely	snake	twisted	windy
misty	pail	reach	softly	under	wing
month	painted	read	soon	uneasy	wisely
moody	patient	really	squid	uneven	with
moon	peace	recent	sun	unhappy	witty
mostly	perfect	regal	tactful	unique	wood
moth	pizza	relax	take	unknown	worthy
music	plaid	remote	tamely	unusual	xebec
musical	plain	restless	tangled	up	xeric
my	plainly	richly	taste	us	xylem
mystery	poetic	roaring	tender	usually	yam
narrow	poorly	rocky	their	vacant	yard
natural	popular	rough	theirs	valley	yearly
near	pretty	roughly	them	vastly	yelp
nearly	proper	round	they	velvet	yield
neatly	proud	rudely	thick	very	yodel
needy	puzzled	run	thorny	vex	yogurt
nervous	quaint	sadly	through	violin	you
never	quash	said	throw	visit	yours
newly	quick	sang	tight	waddle	zany
nicely	quickly	see	timely	warmly	zap
night	quiet	she	timid	we	zeal
normal	quietly	shoe	tiny	wealthy	zealously
off	quill	shouted	tired	weary	zenith
often	radish	shyly	to	weld	zesty
on	ragged	sing	too	well	zipped

Name: _____   Date: _____

Capitalizing Important Words

To **capitalize** means to write the first letter of a word using an uppercase letter.
- Always capitalize the first word of a sentence.
- Capitalize **important words** in names of specific people, places, and things.
- Important words include all nouns, pronouns, verbs, adjectives, and adverbs.
- Unless they are the first word of a sentence or title, do not capitalize: *a, an, the, and, or, but, nor,* or short prepositions, such as *to, of, in, on,* and *at.*
- Capitalize first, last, and middle names of people, including their initials:
    P.T. Barnum   Mary Ann Evans
- Use periods after a person's initials.   *J.P. Morgan*
- Capitalize specific names of animals: *Lassie   Shamu*
- Capitalize a person's title if it is used immediately before a person's name; otherwise it is lowercase.
    Dr. Marian Lipinowski is a dermatologist.
    An apple a day keeps the doctor away.
- Use a period after a title that is abbreviated.
    Dr.   Mrs.   Capt.

Directions: Rewrite these words and phrases correctly.

1. king arthur

_____

2. an English Queen

_____

3. ann brown, president

_____

4. smokey bear

_____

5. judge lawson

_____

6. jumbo, the elephant

_____

7. sir arthur conan doyle

_____

8. president and mrs lincoln

_____

9. the majestic theater

_____

10. mr jrr tolkien

_____

Name: _____ Date: _____

Capitalizing Names

Directions: Fill in the blanks with names of people, animals, or characters as indicated.

1. a man

2. a woman

3. a doctor

4. a relative

5. a teacher

6. an author

7. an animal

8. an athlete

9. a friend

10. a cartoon character

11. another animal

12. yourself

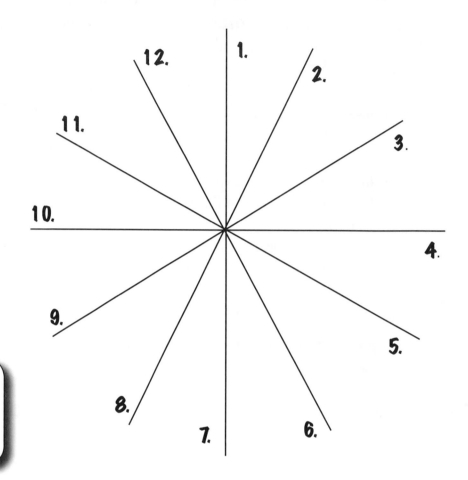

> Many dictionaries indicate words and phrases that should be capitalized. When in doubt, look it up.

Directions: Circle the words that should be capitalized. Add periods where needed.

13. Please join me in welcoming mayor sandra a cummins.

14. Have you met mr peter stone, our next circuit judge?

15. andrew q jorgenson is a professor at the university.

16. prof harlan golfed with dr watson and the governor, thomas j bradley.

17. Why did coach a j brown take the team out for pizza?

18. Have you seen the movie about seabiscuit the racehorse?

19. In the TV show "star trek: the next generation," mr data had a cat named spot.

20. Have you read any books about cinderella, sleeping beauty, or prince charming?

Name: _____ Date: _____

Capitalize and Italicize Titles

Capitalize important words in titles of

- books:
    Harry Potter and the Chamber of Secrets
- newspapers:
    Long Island Reporter
- magazines:
    Sports Illustrated
- plays:
    Romeo and Juliet
- movies:
    The Last of the Mohicans

When you type, use italics for titles of books, newspapers, magazines, plays, and movies. Since you can't write in italics, underline when writing longhand.

Directions: Supply the titles requested below. Underline the titles that should be italicized.

1. Write the title of the last book you read.

_____

2. Name a local newspaper.

_____

3. What magazine do you enjoy reading?

_____

4. Name a play.

_____

5. Write the name of the last movie you saw.

_____

Name: _____   Date: _____

Capitalize With Quotation Marks

Capitalize important words in the titles of
- songs:
  "The Wheels on the Bus"
- poems:
  "Stopping by Woods on a Snowy Evening"
- stories:
  "Snow White and the Seven Dwarfs"
- TV shows:
  "Gilligan's Island"
- articles in newspapers or magazines:
  "Everything You Always Wanted to Know About Capitalization"
- chapters of books:
  "The Worst Birthday"

Enclose titles of TV shows, songs, poems, stories, articles, and chapters inside quotation marks.

Directions: Rewrite these titles. Use correct capitalization and punctuation. Underline or use quotation marks when needed.

1. song: jingle bells _____

2. movie: indiana jones and the temple of doom

_____

3. book: cloudy with a chance of meatballs

_____

4. newspaper: the boston chronicle _____

5. magazine: reader's digest _____

6. article: 101 things you can do to save our planet

_____

7. play: the merchant of venice _____

8. story: the emperor's new clothes _____

9. poem: ode to the west wind _____

10. TV show: ask this old house _____

Name: _____   Date: _____

Capitalize Specific Locations

Capitalize **important words** in the names of

- cities: *Walla Walla*
- counties: *Milwaukee County*
- states and provinces: *Hawaii; Saskatchewan*
- countries: *Turkey; Republic of Haiti*
- continents: *Asia*

Separate the names of cities and states with commas.

Barbourville, Kentucky

Separate the names of cities and countries with commas.

Mexico City, Mexico
The city of Lima, Peru, is the nation's capital.

Directions: Use an atlas. Write the names of three cities and their countries or states for each area on the lines next to the map outline. Then place a dot and the corresponding number on the map. Find names that sound interesting or unusual. Lima, Peru, has been done as an example.

SOUTH AMERICA

1. Lima, Peru _____

2. _____

3. _____

ASIA

1. _____

2. _____

3. _____

SCANDINAVIA

1. _____

2. _____

3. _____

AUSTRALIA

1. _____

2. _____

3. _____

Name: _____   Date: _____

Capitalize Proper Nouns and Adjectives

Capitalize **proper nouns** and **proper adjectives** derived from the names of cities, states, countries, continents, races, languages, nationalities, etc.

Bostonians	*Texans*	*Brazilians*	*Africans*
French	*Spanish*	*Greek*	*English*

Directions: Circle the words that should be capitalized.

1. eun-jung translated the korean story into english and ukrainian.

2. Would you like to play chinese checkers or michigan rummy?

3. We ordered a new york-style pizza with spanish olives, italian sausage, french mushrooms, canadian bacon, bermuda onions, mexican peppers, and greek goat cheese.

4. At the swiss embassy party, guests from several canadian provinces met members of the british parliament, several german actors, and a polish singer.

5. Most people in south america speak spanish.

6. brazil was the only latin american country settled by people from portugal, and portuguese is the official language.

7. My aunt rachel collects persian rugs, arabian horses, and mexican pottery.

8. The egyptian pyramids and the hanging gardens of babylon were two of the seven wonders of the ancient world.

9. When elena researched her family tree, she learned that her ancestors included norwegians, swedes, finns, and russians.

10. Many foods we eat include words derived from cities or countries, such as Turkish taffy, French toast, German rye, and Polish sausage. Write the names of other foods that include the names of places.

_____

_____

_____

Name: _____ Date: _____

What's on the Menu?

Directions: Make capitalization corrections to the menu.

SPECIAL OF THE DAY
denver omelet
with swiss cheese and canadian bacon

SOUP OF THE DAY
new england clam chowder
tex-mex chili

SANDWICHES: meatballs on italian bread
polish sausage on german rye
philly cheese steak

SIDE ORDERS: mashed idaho potatoes
with real lumps
french fries
vidalia onion rings
boston baked beans
texas toast
romaine lettuce salad with
russian dressing, bermuda
onions, and roma tomatoes

DESSERTS: boston cream pie
french vanilla ice cream
georgia peach pie

BEVERAGES: columbian coffee
english tea
florida orange juice

Name: _____ Date: _____

Places, Places

Capitalize **important words** in the names of specific
- planets: *Saturn*
- stars: *Alpha Centari*
- galaxies: *the Milky Way*
- mountain ranges: *the Himalayas*
- valleys: *Pleasant Valley*
- canyons: *Grand Canyon*
- waterfalls: *Bridal Falls*
- rivers: *Mississippi River*
- lakes: *Buffalo Lake*
- volcanoes: *Mount Vesuvius*
- national parks: *Yellowstone National Park*

Words like *mountain* and *lake* are capitalized only when they are part of the name of a specific place.

We climbed several peaks in the <u>Rocky Mountains</u> and the <u>Appalachian Mountains</u>.
We climbed several <u>mountains</u> in the Alps and Himalayas.

We fished in <u>Lake Michigan</u>, <u>Green Lake</u>, and <u>Lake Winnebago</u>.
We fished in several <u>lakes</u> including Erie, Superior, and Huron.

Directions: Circle the capitalization errors.

1. minnesota has 10,000 Lakes.

2. neptune, uranus, mars, and venus are four of the Planets in our solar system.

3. among the longest Rivers on earth are the amazon, the nile, and the mississippi.

4. did you know that earth is in the milky way galaxy?

5. lake titicaca is located on the border between peru and bolivia.

6. the huge statue of christ on mount corcovado overlooks rio de janeiro.

7. thomas jefferson asked lewis and clark to find a water route to the pacific ocean.

8. meriwether lewis and william clark traveled up the missouri river past the great falls.

Name: _____   Date: _____

Addresses

- Capitalize **important words** in the names of streets, avenues, boulevards, etc.

    Avenue of the Americas

- Capitalize words such as *street, lane, route,* and *avenue* <u>only</u> if they are part of a specific address name.

    She lived on <u>Primrose Lane</u>.
    He strolled down the <u>lane</u>.

- Capitalize the two-letter postal abbreviations for states. Do not use a period.

    Boneyard, AZ

Directions: Should the underlined words be capitalized? Write *yes* or *no* on the lines.

1. Hal lived on a busy <u>street</u>. _____

2. Bonnie bought a bungalow on <u>batman boulevard</u>. _____

3. Maureen lives at <u>route</u> 3, Byron, WI. _____

4. The president lives at 1600 <u>pennsylvania avenue</u>. _____

5. Are they building a new <u>highway</u> outside of town? _____

6. My address is 17 <u>crescent circle</u>. _____

7. Send the rebate form to <u>post office box</u> 5493220356475. _____

8. Would you like to live in Toad Suck, <u>ar</u>? _____

9. I can never remember if <u>ak</u> is the abbreviation for Alaska or Arkansas. _____

10. Many of the <u>roads</u> in our county need repair. _____

11. The <u>avenue</u> where Rhonda lives runs east and west. _____

12. Her address is 1213 <u>maple avenue</u>. _____

13. Hannibal, <u>mo</u>, is the hometown of Mark Twain. _____

14. Using the highway is a quicker <u>route</u> than driving down the gravel road. _____

15. Steve lives at 602 <u>highway</u> 95, Brownsville, AL. _____

Name: _____ Date: _____

Abbreviations

- **Abbreviations** are shortened forms of words. Use a period at the end of most abbreviations.

    Mr. is an abbreviation for Mister.

- If the word should be capitalized, then capitalize the abbreviation.

    Is Sesame St. a real street?

- Do not use a period at the end of abbreviations for single words if all letters in the abbreviation are capitalized.

    TV   OK

- Most dictionaries list abbreviations for words.

Directions: Write the abbreviations for the underlined words. Use a dictionary or other reference source if you need help.

1. Main <u>Street</u>   _____

2. Second <u>Avenue</u>   _____

3. Pacific <u>Boulevard</u>   _____

4. Worms, <u>Nebraska</u>   _____

5. <u>Father</u> Flanagan   _____

6. <u>Reverend</u> Jackson   _____

7. <u>Mount Saint</u> Helens   _____

8. <u>Doctor</u> Schweitzer   _____

9. <u>Mistress</u> Abernathy   _____

10. <u>Attorney</u> Rachel Cross   _____

11. 47 <u>South</u> 14th Street   _____

12. <u>Sergeant</u> Smith   _____

13. Columbus <u>Circle</u>   _____

14. Branson, <u>Missouri</u>   _____

15. Windstorm <u>Lane</u>   _____

Name: _____ Date: _____

Special Days

> Capitalize
>
> - names of days of the week:
>   *Monday*
> - names of the months:
>   *February*
> - important words in holidays:
>   *Fourth of July*

Directions: Circle the words that should be capitalized.

1.	january	new year's day	feast of the three kings	chocolate cake day
2.	february	valentine's day	groundhog day	presidents' day
3.	march	st. patrick's day	mardi gras	easter sunday
4.	april	all fools' day	passover	earth day
5.	may	mother's day	memorial day	armed forces day
6.	june	father's day	flag day	american eagle day
7.	july	independence day	canada day	aunt and uncle day
8.	august	sisters' day	lefthander's day	tell a joke day
9.	september	labor day	grandparents' day	international day of peace
10.	october	columbus day	halloween	yom kippur
11.	november	thanksgiving day	veterans' day	square dancing day
12.	december	christmas day	hanukkah	kwanzaa

Riddle Me

Directions: Circle all words that should be capitalized. Can you answer the riddles?

1. which hand do people in iowa use to eat their soup?

2. why can't a man living in new york be buried west of the mississippi river?

3. if milk is $2.75 a gallon in illinois, what are window panes in missouri?

4. where do math teachers like to visit in new york city?

5. for what should you be thankful on thanksgiving day?

6. before mount everest was discovered, what was the tallest mountain in the world?

7. when does friday come before thursday?

8. on january 1 at 7:15 a.m., fourteen people walked out of the best restaurant in paris, france. Why?

9. in what month do coyotes howl the least?

10. if april showers bring may flowers, then what do may flowers bring?

11. why did santa have only seven reindeer on christmas eve?

12. what do cows in wisconsin do for fun on a saturday night?

13. a man in texas wore red shoes every day for a year. What did they become when he stepped into the rio grande river?

14. a man rode into tombstone, arizona, on his horse. He arrived on friday, spent three days in town, and left on friday. How is this possible?

15. what do people in devonshire, england, call baby cats?

16. which candles burn longer: white ones in spain or blue ones in germany?

17. why did cowboys in new mexico ride their horses to town?

Name: _____ Date: _____

Acronyms

- **Acronyms** are words made from the first letters of a group of words. Usually the word is pronounced by saying the name of each letter.
- Capitalize all letters in acronyms. Do not use periods.

Directions: Use a dictionary or other reference source to complete the acronym chart.

	Acronym	Meaning
1.	ASAP	as soon as possible
2.	_____	Central Intelligence Agency
3.	_____	cash on delivery
4.	GI	_____
5.	IRS	_____
6.	NBC	_____
7.	_____	National Football League
8.	PM	_____
9.	PS	_____
10.	_____	registered nurse
11.	RV	_____
12.	_____	self-contained underwater breathing apparatus
13.	_____	unidentified flying object
14.	_____	very important person

Sometimes small words are omitted in acronyms.

15.	BLT	bacon, lettuce, and tomato
16.	FBI	_____
17.	NASA	_____

Name: _____   Date: _____

More Words to Capitalize

Directions: Fill in the blanks with another example of each type.

Capitalize important words in the names of:

- political parties: Democrats   _____

- religious groups: Latter-Day Saints   _____

- formal groups: Knights of Columbus   _____

- organizations: Girl Scouts   _____

- schools: Adams Middle School   _____

- universities   University of Maine   _____

- colleges   Boston College   _____

- monuments: Lincoln Memorial   _____

- famous buildings: Empire State Building   _____

- ships: U.S.S. *Arizona*   _____

- computer programs/software: Adobe Reader™   _____

- government departments: Department of Justice   _____

- famous documents: Bill of Rights   _____

- major historical periods   the Middle Ages   _____

- major events in history: the Great Depression   _____

- wars: Revolutionary War   _____

- battles: Battle of Gettysburg   _____

Name: _____ Date: _____

Odds and Ends

- Capitalize the first word in the **salutation** of a letter:
  Dear Mary,

- Capitalize the first word in the **closing** of a letter:
  Yours truly,

- Capitalize the important words in brand names and use the trademark symbol:
  Colgate™

- Capitalize important words in the nicknames of people, animals, places, or things:
  King of Swat   *Rex, the Wonder Dog*
  City of Angels   *Old Faithful*

Directions: Underline the words that should be capitalized.

dear sid,

did you see the baseball history special on tv last night? my favorite story was the one about "shoeless" joe jackson. he began his baseball career as a pitcher but became an outfielder because his fast ball was so forceful it once broke a catcher's arm, and nobody would agree to catch for him.

you knew I was named for stan "the man" musial, the famous right fielder and first baseman for the st. louis cardinals, didn't you? my middle name, louis, came from the "iron horse," lou gehrig.

my dad played minor-league ball for a while and has always been a great baseball fan. he couldn't decide whether to name me ty, after the "georgia peach," ty cobb, or joe, after "joltin'" joe dimaggio. mom refused to consider the name george for george herman ruth because she thought a nickname like "babe" wouldn't be all that great when I grew up.

maybe this summer we can head up to the windy city and watch the cubbies play at wrigley field.

your cousin,

stan

Name: _____ Date: _____

Proofread the Trivia

Directions: Circle the words that need to be capitalized in the following sentences. The number of errors is included in brackets ([ ]) at the end of each sentence.

1. people who live in naples, italy, are called neopolitans. [4]

2. some cities with unusual names include embarrass, mn; square butt, mt; and echo, tx. [8]

3. did you know that the full name of the wonderful cartoon duck created by walt disney was donald fauntleroy duck? [6]

4. some of the villains in the tv show "batman" included king tut, the joker, the archer, the black widow, the mad hatter, and the clock king. [13]

5. adam west played the part of batman, and burt ward played his sidekick, robin, the boy wonder. [8]

6. andy griffith, better known as sheriff andy taylor, never won an emmy for either of his popular tv shows: "the andy griffith show" or "matlock." [12]

7. don knotts, who played deputy barney fife, won five emmys for his supporting role. [6]

8. before lassie became the heroine of a popular tv show, she was the main character in a short novel titled, *lassie come home*, written by eric mowbray knight. [9]

9. caryn johnson made her first appearance on stage at the helena rubenstein children's theatre in new york city at the age of 8. [9]

10. you may not recognize the name caryn johnson, but you might know her by her stage name, whoopi goldberg. [5]

Name: _____ Date: _____

End Punctuation

All sentences end with punctuation.

- Sentences that state a fact or a command end with a **period**.

  Gorillas rarely wash their hands after eating.
  Wash the gorilla's hands before you leave, Glen.

- Sentences that ask a question end with a **question mark**.

  Glen, did you remember to wash the gorilla's hands?

- Sentences that show strong emotion or surprise end with an **exclamation point**.

  Wow! That gorilla has really clean hands!

Directions: Add punctuation to the end of each sentence. Circle all the words where there is a capitalization error.

1. Who gave the zebra a bath

2. Oh, oh! Look what happened

3. Paint the stripes on the zebras before you go to lunch

4. Did you know that a hippopotamus can run faster than a person

5. The word *hippopotamus* means "water horse" in greek

6. Hummingbirds can fly backwards

7. fill the hummingbird feeder with sugar water

8. Look, There are six hummingbirds at the feeder already

9. Do you know which land animal is the tallest

10. At birth, a baby giraffe is six feet tall

11. That's a very tall baby

12. giraffes were called "camel leopards" by the Romans

Name: _____ Date: _____

Commas Separate

- Use a **comma** to separate the number of the day of the month and the year.

  Abraham Lincoln was born on February 12, 1809.
  December 7, 1941, was the date of the attack on Pearl Harbor.

- Do not use a comma to separate the month and year if no date is given.

  George Washington was born in February 1732.

- Use **commas** to separate three or more words in a series.

  Mia ordered spaghetti, garlic bread, a salad, and a soda.

- Use a **comma** to separate cities from states, provinces, and/or other countries.

  Monkey's Eyebrow, Kentucky
  Attawapiskat, Ontario, Canada
  Rome, Italy
  Jefferson City, Missouri, is the capital of the state.

Directions: Add commas to the following sentences.

1. Thomas Jefferson, born on April 13 1743, in Shadwell Virginia, became the third president in March 1801.

2. Jefferson died on July 4 1826, and was buried at his home near Charlottesville Virginia.

3. Born in Hyde Park New Jersey in January 1882, Franklin D. Roosevelt died on April 12 1945, shortly after he began his fourth term as president.

4. Three different men served as vice president with Franklin Roosevelt: John N. Garner Henry A. Wallace and Harry S Truman.

5. While president, Richard M. Nixon traveled to Moscow Russia, and Beijing China.

6. Theodore Roosevelt had six children: Alice Theodore Kermit Ethel Archibald and Quentin.

Commas With Direct Address and Appositives

- Use **commas** to separate nouns or pronouns in **direct address** from the rest of the sentence. A noun or pronoun in direct address is one that names or refers to the person addressed.

  Glen, your gorilla is a disgrace!
  Your gorilla, Glen, is a disgrace!
  Your gorilla is a disgrace, Glen!

- Use **commas** to separate appositives from the rest of the sentence. **Appositives** are words that provide more information about a previous noun or pronoun.

  Glen, the boy with the pet gorilla, is my neighbor.

Directions: Underline the noun or pronoun used in direct address. Add commas where needed.

1. Barry you have to get over your barophobia if you ever hope to become an astronaut.

2. Listen, Barry barophobia means fear of gravity.

3. Do you have any other phobias Barry?

4. "Santa Claus I'd like you to meet my friend, Jeanine," said the littlest elf.

5. "Jeanine might be shy Santa because she has pogonophobia, a fear of beards," he explained.

Directions: Underline the word or words used as appositives. Add commas where needed.

6. Boston the city sometimes called Bean Town is the capital of Massachusetts.

7. Calvin Coolidge known as Silent Cal installed a mechanical horse in the White House and liked to bounce around on it, whooping like a cowboy at a rodeo.

8. Harriet Tubman nicknamed the "Moses of her people" led many slaves to freedom on the Underground Railroad.

9. Besides being a writer and a politician, Benjamin Franklin the man who invented bifocals also invented lightning rods.

10. Acrophobia the fear of heights is rather common, but alektorophobia the fear of chickens is quite rare.

Name: _____   Date: _____

Commas With Independent Clauses

- Use a **comma** to separate independent clauses in a compound sentence joined by the words *and, for, or, nor,* or *but.*

- An **independent clause** is a group of words that makes a complete thought. Each independent clause could be a complete sentence by itself.

  Doug ate a cheese pizza for lunch, and he ordered a cup of raspberry cappuccino to go, but he decided to play hooky, and he did not return to his office.

- If the independent clauses are very short (two or three words), a comma is not needed.

  He told jokes but she didn't laugh.

Directions: Join the independent clauses to make one sentence joined by *and, for, or, nor,* or *but.* Rewrite the sentences using commas where needed.

1. Abby raked the leaves into piles. Andy put the leaves into bags.

_____

_____

2. Beth wanted to spend the day at the mall. She also wanted to spend the day at the beach.

_____

_____

3. Carlos fixed my bicycle. He could not fix my car.

_____

_____

4. Diane ate three helpings of spaghetti for supper. She was too full for dessert.

_____

_____

5. Ethan ran a good race. Ellen finished in first place.

_____

_____

6. Chuck washed the windows of his '57 Chevy. He checked the oil. He forgot to fill it with gas.

_____

_____

Name: _____ Date: _____

A Few More Ways to Use Commas

- Use a comma after the **salutation** in a friendly letter.

  Dear John,

- Use a comma after the **closing** in a letter.

  Your friend,

- Use a comma after **introductory phrases**.

  After Consuela finished sweeping, the wind began to blow.

- The meaning of a sentence can completely change if commas are missing. A comma is used to show that Consuela did not sweep the wind in the sentence above. Without a comma in the following sentence, it would seem that Marco ate the sea gulls.

  As Marco ate, the sea gulls circled, waiting for crumbs.

- Use a comma after **yes or no** when it is the first word in a sentence.

  Yes, Abraham Lincoln was born in a log cabin.
  No, George Washington didn't chop down a cherry tree.

Directions: Add commas where needed.

1. When we cooked the people in the apartment next to us complained about the smell.

2. When we barbecued the neighbor's dog barked.

3. While the children ate the horses grazed.

4. If grandma bakes the children will have homemade gingerbread for dessert.

5. No we aren't in Kansas anymore.

6. Before you vacuum the goldfish bowl should be cleaned.

7. Dear Santa

8. Yours truly

9. Since Dave left the house seems much quieter.

10. Because Kathy stopped the turtle was not crushed by the car.

Name: _____ Date: _____

Quotations

- A **quotation** contains the exact words written or spoken by someone. Quotation marks show when the person's words begin and end.

  Comedian Groucho Marx once said, "Outside of a dog, a book is man's best friend. Inside of a dog, it's too dark to read."

- Use a **comma** to set off words such as *he said* and *she replied* that are not part of the quotation.

  Snoopy said, "Yesterday, I was a dog. Today, I'm a dog. Tomorrow, I'll probably still be a dog. Sigh! There's so little hope for advancement."

- If a quotation is a **complete sentence**, put end-of-sentence punctuation inside the quotation marks.

  Douglas Adams, author of <u>Hitchhiker's Guide to the Galaxy</u>, wrote, "The ships hung in the sky in much the same way that bricks don't."

- If a quotation is **not complete**, put a comma inside the quotation marks, followed by the rest of the quotation.

  "Show me a sane man," said Carl Jung, "and I will cure him for you."

Directions: Use the examples above as guidelines. Add quotation marks, commas, and end-of-sentence punctuation as needed.

1. After serving one term as president, Calvin Coolidge stated I do not choose to run for President in 1928

2. When asked why, Coolidge replied Because there's no chance for advancement

3. There, I guess King George will be able to read that stated John Hancock after he signed his name in large letters on the Declaration of Independence.

4. People who are wrapped up in themselves make small packages wrote Benjamin Franklin.

5. Now that I realize what they've had to put up with wrote Betty Ford about being the first lady I have a new respect and admiration for every one of them

Name: _____ Date: _____

Yogi-isms

Directions: Yogi Berra was a baseball catcher, manager, and coach. He was a member of the Baseball Hall of Fame, and he was famous for his unusual sayings. Add the correct punctuation to these quotes.

1. A nickel ain't worth a dime anymore he complained

2. It's never happened in World Series history, and it hasn't happened since Yogi told fans

3. It's déjà vu all over again he exclaimed

4. Yogi advised When you come to a fork in the road, take it

5. He also said We're lost but we're making good time

6. If I didn't wake up I'd still be sleeping he said

7. Some of Yogi's advice was confusing, like the time he said Always go to other people's funerals; otherwise, they won't go to yours

8. Little League baseball is a good thing 'cause it keeps the parents off the streets and it keeps the kids out of the house! he told a reporter

9. The future ain't what it used to be Yogi said, and I think he was right

10. Yogi once said I never said most of the things I said

11. You've got to be very careful if you don't know where you are going, because you might not get there was one of Yogi's quotes that left people scratching their heads

12. Pair up in threes he told the players

13. Yogi said I usually take a two-hour nap from one to four so it was hard to know when he would be awake

14. We made too many wrong mistakes Yogi explained

15. Try to remember that Yogi advised if the world were perfect, it wouldn't be

Name: _____ Date: _____

Proofreading

Directions: First, circle the letter of the sentence in each group that is completely correct. Then, briefly describe the punctuation error found in each of the other sentences in the group.

Group 1

A. Jake, woke suddenly in the middle of a dark and stormy night.

_____

B. Thunder boomed and lightning flashed!

_____

C. What were those sounds coming from his closet.

_____

D. Jake reached for his glasses but he could not find them.

_____

Group 2

A. Meanwhile, the small furry creature trapped in the closet tried to get Jake's attention.

_____

B. Let me out, it called in small furry creature talk.

_____

C. Lightning flared casting strange shadows on the walls and ceiling.

_____

D. Thunder shook the house?

_____

Group 3

A. After the thunder the silence seemed ominous.

_____

B. When Jake finally found his glasses and switched on the lamp beside his bed he found himself in a strange room.

_____

C. His bed his dresser his posters and even his stinky dirty clothes were gone.

_____

D. "Let me out of here!" boomed a loud voice from behind a door near the bed.

_____

Name: _____   Date: _____

Contractions

- A **contraction** contains two words joined together to make a shorter word.
  there is = there's
- Use an **apostrophe** to show one or more missing letters.
  you have = you've
- Many contractions contain a pronoun and a verb.
  we would = we'd
- Some **contractions** include a verb and the word *not*.
  should not = shouldn't

Directions: Complete the pronoun/verb contractions below.

	Pronoun	Verb		Contraction
1.	I	+ am	=	I'm
2.	we	+ are	=	we're
	you	+ are	=	you're
	they	+ are	=	_____
3.	he	+ is	=	he's
	she	+ is	=	_____
	it	+ is	=	it's
4.	I	+ have	=	I've
	we	+ have	=	_____
	you	+ have	=	you've
	they	+ have	=	_____
5.	I	+ would	=	I'd
	you	+ would	=	_____
	we	+ would	=	we'd
	she	+ would	=	_____
	he	+ would	=	he'd
	they	+ would	=	_____
6.	I	+ will	=	_____
	you	+ will	=	_____
	we	+ will	=	_____
	she	+ will	=	_____
	he	+ will	=	_____
	they	+ will	=	_____

Directions: Finish the verb/not contractions below.

7. did + not = _____

8. should + not = _____

9. had + not = _____

10. will + not = _____

11. _____ + _____ = wouldn't

12. _____ + _____ = couldn't

13. _____ + _____ = haven't

14. _____ + _____ = shan't

15. _____ + _____ = can't

Invincible Picture

IT COULDN'T HAVE HAPPENED

Name: _____ Date: _____

Write the Contractions

Directions: Write the contractions for the underlined words.

1. Rocky and Moose <u>are not</u> going to the apiary because they have

apiphobia, a fear of bees. _____

2. <u>I have</u> never heard of anyone having arachibutyrophobia, a fear of

peanut butter sticking to the roof of one's mouth. _____

3. <u>He is</u> never going to become an astronaut because he has siderophobia, a fear of the stars,

and cometophobia, a fear of comets. _____

4. Abby <u>will not</u> march in the parade because she has aulophobia, a fear of flutes.

_____

5. Who <u>would have</u> thought that a librarian could develop bibliophobia, a fear of books?

_____

6. By the time Anne finishes cleaning her room, <u>she will</u> have blennophobia, a fear of slime.

_____

7. I know Samantha <u>does not</u> have catoptrophobia, a fear of mirrors.

_____

8. <u>Do not</u> move to Alaska if you have chionophobia, a fear of snow, or cryophobia, a fear of ice

or frost. _____

9. <u>You had</u> better not move to an island if you have gephyrophobia, a fear of crossing bridges.

_____

10. The twins always stay together because <u>they are</u> afraid of empty rooms. (kenophobia)

_____

11. People who want to become mechanics <u>should not</u> have mechanophobia, a fear of machinery.

_____

12. <u>What is</u> his problem? <u>It is</u> called tonitrophobia and means a fear of thunder.

_____ _____

Name: _____ Date: _____

Apostrophes With Singular Possessives

- Use an **apostrophe** to show possession when writing about something that belongs to someone or something.

- If the noun is singular, add an apostrophe and an *s* at the end of the word.
  frog's fur   *Ross's* rhinoceros

- The word that names what is owned can be singular or plural.
  A singular noun with one item:
  the lady's lizard   (One lady has one lizard.)

  A singular noun with more than one item:
  the lady's leopards   (One lady has more than one leopard.)

- If using the possessive form of a noun sounds weird or wrong, as in number 9 below, you can reword your sentence using a possessive pronoun.

  Correct, but awkward: *The mouse's houses were inside the wall.*

  Rewritten using a possessive pronoun: *The mouse had its houses inside the wall.*

Directions: Rewrite the phrases using the possessive form of the noun. The first one is done as an example.

1. one man has more than one monkey:

   man's monkeys
   _____

2. Oscar has one orange octopus:

   _____

3. Dr. Seuss has more than one story:

   _____

4. a child has several grandparents:

   _____

5. Agnes has more than one ache:

   _____

6. a fly has more than one wing:

   _____

7. a zebra has more than one stripe:

   _____

8. Pat has one pair of pajamas:

   _____

9. a mouse has more than one house:

   _____

10. a goose has more than one egg:

   _____

Name: _____ Date: _____

Apostrophes With Plural Possessives

- Use an **apostrophe** to show possession when writing about something that belongs to someone or something.

- If the noun is plural and ends in an *s,* add an apostrophe at the end of the word.
  the <u>boys'</u> team

- If the noun is plural and does not end in an *s,* add an apostrophe and an *s.*
  the <u>people's</u> choice

- The word that names what is owned can be singular or plural.
  Plural noun with one item that belongs to all of them:
  the <u>children's</u> mother   (more than one child with the same mother)

  Plural noun with more than one item:
  the <u>ladies'</u> gardens   (more than one lady and more than one garden)

- If using the possessive form of a noun sounds weird or wrong, as in number 8 below, you can reword your sentence.

  Correct, but awkward: *The mice's houses were inside the wall.*

  Rewritten using a possessive pronoun: *The mice had their houses inside the wall.*

Directions: Rewrite the phrases using the possessive form of the noun.

1. more than one goose has more than one egg:

_____

2. one woman belonging to several clubs:

_____

3. more than one woman belonging to one club:

_____

4. more than one bird with more than one nest:

_____

5. grandparents with more than one grandchild:

_____

6. one fly with more than one eye:

_____

7. more than one fly has more than one eye:

_____

8. more than one mouse having more than one house:

_____

Name: _____ Date: _____

Possessive Pronouns

- **Possessive pronouns** take the place of possessive nouns.
    Amy lost <u>Amy's</u> dog.
    Amy lost <u>her</u> dog.

- Do not use an apostrophe to show possession with pronouns. Instead, use the possessive form of the pronoun.

    Possessive pronouns are:

Singular	**Plural**
my, mine	*our, ours*
your, yours	*your, yours*
his, her, hers, its	*their, theirs*

Directions: Write possessive pronouns to complete the sentences correctly.

1. That apple is Ashley's. It is _____.

2. Ashley took a bite of _____ apple.

3. I bought a CD player. It is _____.

4. I brought _____ CD player to the party.

5. You won the contest, so the prize is _____.

6. When you leave, don't forget to take _____ prize.

7. The dog chased _____ tail, but it did not catch it.

8. Eduardo left _____ new baseball mitt outside in the rain.

9. On the way to the party, they lost _____ pet snake.

10. If you find a lost snake, you will know it is _____.

Name: _____ Date: _____

Contractions and Possessive Pronouns

- Don't confuse contractions with possessive pronouns.

    Contractions

    It's means *it is*.   You're means *you are*.

    They're means *they are*.   There's means *there is*.

    Possessive Pronouns

    Its means something *belongs to it*.

    Your means something *belongs to you*.

    Their means something *belongs to them*.

    Theirs means it *belongs to them*.

Directions: Circle the correct words to complete each sentence.

1. (It's, Its) time for the dog to take (it's, its) medicine.

2. (Your, You're) going to get (your, you're) reward soon.

3. (Their, They're) lending us (their, they're) DVD player.

4. The problem is (theirs, there's), and (theirs, there's) no one who can help.

Directions: Write possessive pronouns or contractions in the blanks to finish the sentences.

5. _____ too bad that your dog is sick.

6. Have you taken _____ dog to the vet?

7. _____ a new vet on Main Street.

8. Is your dog too sick to wag _____ tail?

9. I'm sure _____ worried about it.

10. Most dog owners become concerned when _____ pets are ill.

11. Max and Frieda were very upset when _____ had to stay at the animal hospital overnight.

12. Aren't you glad the vet said _____ nothing seriously wrong with your dog?

Name: _____ Date: _____

Introducing: The Colon

- The main purpose of a **colon** is to introduce something.
- A **colon** can introduce a word, a phrase, a sentence, or a list.

    Jamal had only one thing on his mind: winning. (a word)

    Jamal had only one thing on his mind: winning the game. (a phrase)

    Jamal had only one thing on his mind: he wanted to win the game. (a sentence)

    Jamal had three things on his mind: finding a receiver, passing the ball, and scoring points. (a list)

Directions: Insert colons where needed. Not all sentences will need colons.

1. For years Jan had saved her money for a reason to take a trip to Hawaii.

2. Jan knew exactly what she wanted to do in Hawaii visit a volcano, swim in the ocean, and visit a pineapple plantation.

3. When Jan visited the island of Oahu, she couldn't believe what she saw a gigantic windmill with blades 400 feet long!

4. Jan tried a new food that she really enjoyed *poi*, a type of dip popular in Hawaii and the South Pacific.

5. To make *poi*, these ingredients are cooked together sweet potatoes and bananas or taro root.

6. After cooking the ingredients until they are soft, *poi* is mashed with water.

7. Traditionally, after preparing *poi*, Hawaiians allow it to sit for a few days until it ferments and turns sour.

8. Jan learned this fact about our fiftieth state more than one-third of the world's pineapple is grown in Hawaii.

9. Coffee is grown in only one of the fifty states Hawaii.

10. Three states do not change over to daylight saving time Arizona, Indiana, and Hawaii.

Name: _____   Date: _____

Five More Ways to Use a Colon

- Use a **colon** after the **salutation** of a business letter.

  Dear Sir:

- Use a **colon** between the hour and the minute when writing time.

  School ends at 3:30.

- Use a **colon** between chapters and verses of the Bible.

  "Friends always show their love. What are brothers for if not to share troubles?" (Proverbs 17:17)

- Use a **colon** to separate the act from the scene of a play.

  My favorite scene from a Shakespearean play is the one with the three witches in Macbeth I:1.

- Use a **colon** to separate the title from the subtitle of a book.

  Have you ever read <u>The Story of Harriet Tubman: Conductor of the Underground Railroad</u> ?

Directions: Circle the incorrect punctuation and insert a colon instead.

1. Meet me at 11–55, and we'll head for the mall.

2. "An honest answer is the sign of true friendship." (Proverbs 24,26)

3. I enjoyed reading *Seabiscuit. An American Legend.*

4. Dear Mr. President,

5. "Be not afraid of greatness. Some are born great, some achieve greatness, and some have greatness thrust upon 'em." (*Twelfth Night* II,5)

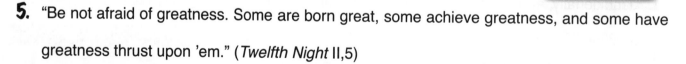

Directions: Use the Internet or other reference sources to find a quotation from a play or the Bible. Write the quotation and its source. Use quotation marks and a colon.

6. _____

_____

_____

Name: _____ Date: _____

Semicolons

- A **semicolon** signals a reader to pause longer than for a comma, but not as long as for a period. You could call it a "super comma."

- Use a **semicolon** to connect closely related independent clauses not joined by *and, or, nor, for, yet,* or *but*. Often the second clause makes a comment on the first clause.

  An **independent clause** is a group of words that makes a complete thought. Each independent clause could be a complete sentence by itself.

  She lost her marbles; he found them.
  The film was excellent; it won many awards.

  Remember, when two independent clauses are joined by a conjunction (*and, or, nor, for, yet,* or *but*), use a comma.

Directions: Insert a comma or semicolon to separate the independent clauses in each sentence.

1. Little Bo Peep had three sheep but she lost them.

2. She left them alone they came back home.

3. Mary had a little lamb it followed her to school.

4. The mouse ran up the clock and the clock struck one.

5. The little dog laughed the dish ran away with the spoon.

6. The sheep are in the meadow and the cows are in the corn.

7. Jack be nimble Jack be quick.

8. Jack and Jill went up the hill and then they tumbled down.

9. In her garden, she grew silver bells and cockleshells but she didn't grow any oats, peas, beans, or barley.

10. There once was a woman who lived in a shoe yet she and her children lived happily ever after.

Name: _____ Date: _____

Dashes and Semicolons

- A **semicolon** is a super comma between items in a list that already contains commas.

    The rock group played in Little Rock, Arkansas; Rockford, Illinois; Lone Rock, Texas; Slippery Rock, Pennsylvania; and Rock Springs, Wyoming.

- Use a **dash** (—) to separate words in the middle of a sentence to indicate a sudden change of thought.

    I want a hot dog—no, make that a hamburger—for lunch.

- Use a **dash** (—) to attach material to the end of a sentence when there is a clean break in continuity.

    Wear your old clothes—new ones might get spoiled.

- **Caution:** Use dashes sparingly.

Directions: Review the uses of colons, semicolons, and dashes, and then insert them correctly in the following.

1. I'll pick you up at 730 no make it 710 and we'll go rock climbing.

2. The pilot flew to Rome, Italy Frankfurt, Germany Paris, France and London, England last week.

3. Let's follow the west trail or would you rather not?

4. All the people from the village men, women, children joined the animals fleeing the out-of-control fire.

5. Lincoln was a tall man who wore a top hat a most unusual sight to be sure.

6. I'd like a chocolate shake better make that a diet soda. I'm trying to lose weight.

7. Dear Library Director

8. Would you please order more historical fiction like *The Black Flower A Novel of the Civil War* for our library?

Name: _____ Date: _____

Punctuation Review

Directions: Write a short sentence about plants, trees, or flowers using the type of punctuation listed.

Quotation marks _____

_____

_____

Question mark _____

_____

Apostrophe _____

_____

Colon _____

_____

Comma _____

_____

Exclamation point _____

_____

Semicolon _____

_____

_____

Dash _____

_____

Answer Keys

Nouns (p. 2)
1. ball; dimples
2. sharks; fish; eyes
3. 1927; service; New York; London; $75.00; minutes
4. telephones; 1899
5. yo-yo; invention; children; Rome; toys; wood; metal; years

Singular and Plural Nouns (p. 3)
1. leaves
2. flies
3. trophies
4. elves
5. hippopotamuses or hippopotami
6. skies
7. buses or busses
8. oxen
9. addresses
10. boxes

11–20. Answers will vary. Possible answers are listed.
11. answers
12. children
13. enemies
14. nights
15. floors
16. freedom
17. frown

Irregular Noun Plurals (p. 4)
1. men
2. women
3. geese
4. lice
5. scissors
6. sheep
7. moose
8. teeth
9. feet
10. fish or fishes
11. cattle
12. data
13. crises
14. bacteria
15. analyses
16. pants
17. fungi
18. indexes or indices
19. foci
20. appendixes or appendices

Proper Nouns (p. 5)
1. George Washington; Thomas Jefferson; Abraham Lincoln; Theodore Roosevelt; Mount Rushmore; Black Hills; South Dakota; Gutzon Borglum
2. Yellowstone National Park; Wyoming; Montana; Idaho; President Ulysses S. Grant
3. Maine; Maryland; Massachusetts; Michigan; Minnesota; Mississippi; Missouri; Montana
4. Harriet Tubman; Moses; Underground Railroad
5. Thanksgiving; Thursday; November

6–9. Answers will vary.

Action Verbs (p. 6)
Answers will vary.

Singular and Plural Verbs (p. 7)
1. play
2. guesses
3. coughs
4. wish
5. growl
6. drives
7. display
8. think
9. waxes
10. dances

11. P, fear
12. P, try; lick
13. P, sleep
14. S, rigged; could open
15. S, runs
16. S, can run
17. P, suffer
18. S, means

Verbs of Being (p. 8)
1. Pizza — tastes — great
2. Frankenstein — felt — hungry
3. Dinner — smells — delicious
4. Spencer — Did appear — sad
5. zebra — is — white
6. Grandpa — Did feel — sleepy
7. They — were — elated
8. sister — grew — taller
9. You — seem — worried
10. Hippopotomonstrosesquippedaliophobia — is — fear

Verb Tense (p. 9)
1. PA; washed
2. PA; named
3. PR; takes
4. F; will learn
5. PR; loves
6. PA; hibernated
7. PA; did hibernate
8. F; will see
9. F; can come
10. PA; came

11–13. Answers will vary.

Three Forms of Verbs (p. 10)
1. sailed; had sailed
2. mopped; had mopped
3. emptied; had emptied
4. jumped; had jumped
5. tried; had tried
6. believed; had believed
7. sipped; had sipped
8. fried; had fried
9. pushed; had pushed
10. implied; had implied
11. moped; had moped
12. planted; had planted

Irregular Verbs (p. 11)
1. ridden
2. thrown
3. caught
4. grown
5. go
6. went
7. seen
8. bought

Complete Sentences (p. 12)
1. yes
2. no
3. no
4. yes
5. no

6–7. Answers will vary.

Kinds of Sentences (p. 13)
1–8. Answers will vary.
9. question mark   10. period
11. exclamation point   12. period

Simple Predicates (p. 14)
1. A; ate   2. A; danced
3. A; would pass   4. A; arrived
5. B; is   6. A; A; baked; ate
7. A; A; traveled; rode   8. B; are
9. B; is   10. B; B; have; do have
11–12. Answers will vary.

Simple Subjects (p. 15)
1. wolf   2. you; Little Boy Blue
3. Jack   4. cow
5. dish   6. mouse
7. Jack; Jill   8. oats; peas; beans; barley
9. Jack; Mary
10. Old King Cole; fiddlers; Knave; mice
11–14. Answers will vary.

Agreement of Subjects and Predicates (p. 16)
Verbs will vary.
1. P; lizards, snakes   2. S; Everyone
3. S; Chili   4. P; squirrel, snail, skunk
5. S; pig   6. S; money
7. S; anyone   8. S; village
Nouns will vary.
9. P   10. S   11. S   12. P
13. S   14. S   15. P

Pronouns as Subjects (p. 17)
1. It   2. He   3. It
4. They   5. She   6. We
7–12. Answers will vary.

Possessive Pronouns (p. 18)
1. her; hers   2. my; mine
3. his; his   4. our; ours
5. their; theirs   6. your; yours
7. its   8. your; yours
9. its   10. my; mine
11. her; hers   12. their; theirs
13. his; his   14. our; ours

Contractions and Possessive Pronouns (p. 19)
1. You're   2. your
3. theirs   4. There's
5. It's, your   6. They're
7. their   8. its
9–12. Answers will vary.

Direct and Indirect Objects (p. 20)
1. pizza, cake, ice cream
2. room, streamers
3. leaves
4. song, flowers
5. bike, motorcycle
6. Pedro   haircut
7. Todd, Tami   gift
8. Randy, Lynn $20.00
9. Andy, Tori   story
10. Heather   trick
11. baby   lullaby
12. Devin   book

Interrogative Pronouns (p. 21)
1. Which or What   2. Who   3. Whose
4. whom   5. which   6. what
7. Whose or Which or What   8. whom

Adjectives (p. 22)
Answers will vary.

Comparative and Superlative Adjectives (p. 23)
Answers will vary. Please be certain that students use the comparative or superlative form as indicated.
1. comparative   2. superlative
3. comparative   4. superlative
5. comparative   6. superlative
7. comparative   8. comparative
9. comparative   10. superlative
11. comparative   12. superlative

Comparative and Superlative Forms of Longer Adjectives (p. 24)
1. floppier; floppiest   2. slower; slowest
3. more expensive; most expensive
4. happier; happiest   5. later; latest
6. heavier; heaviest   7. farther; farthest
8. worse; worst   9. more; most
10. better; best   11. worse; worst
12. less; least

Adverbs (p. 25)
2. eagerly drove
3. completely filled
4. far traveled
5. tomorrow will arrive
6. quietly played
7. Too soon; soon began
8. eventually became; very slippery
Teacher check questions.

Comparative and Superlative Adverbs (p. 26)
Answers will vary.
1. comparative
2. superlative
3. comparative
4. comparative
5. comparative
6. comparative
7. comparative
8. superlative
9. comparative
10. superlative

Adjective or Adverb? (p. 27)
Explanations will vary.
1. ADJ
2. ADV
3. ADJ
4. ADV
5. ADJ
6. ADJ
7. ADV
8. ADJ
9. ADV
10. ADJ

Prepositions and Prepositional Phrases (p. 28)
Fill-in-the-blank answers will vary.
1. circus
2. tree
3. inside
4. without
5. past, mountains
6. rooftops
7. forest
8. near, castle
9. of

Identifying Prepositions and Prepositional Phrases (p. 29)
2. (in the hand) (in the bush)
3. (of a thousand miles) (with a single step)
4. (in glass houses)
5. (in the mouth)
6. (on the other side) (of the fence)
7. (in a day)
8. (of a feather)
9. (of invention)
10. (from little acorns)
11. (from a sow's ear)
12. (under the bridge)

Objective Pronouns (p. 30)
Pronouns will vary.
1. DO
2. DO
3. OP
4. IO
5. OP
6. IO; IO
7. OP; OP
8. IO
9. DO
10. OP

Homophones (p. 31)
1. sails (verb); week (noun)
2. wait (verb); to (preposition)
3. sale (noun)
4. pair (noun); cents (noun)
5. red (adjective); blue (adjective)
6. brakes (noun)
7. way (noun); made (verb); right (adjective); Maine (noun)
8. stare (verb); fur (adjective)
9. pale (adjective); flu (noun)
10. knew (verb); four (noun); two (noun); know (verb); one (noun); eight (noun)

Conjunctions (p. 32)
1. but
2. and/so
3. or
4. because
5. or
6. so
7. and
8–10. Answers will vary.

More Than One Part of Speech (p. 33)
Answers will vary.

Capitalizing Important Words (p. 37)
1. King Arthur
2. an English queen
3. Ann Brown, president
4. Smokey Bear
5. Judge Lawson
6. Jumbo, the elephant
7. Sir Arthur Conan Doyle
8. President and Mrs. Lincoln
9. the Majestic Theater
10. Mr. J.R.R. Tolkien

Capitalizing Names (p. 38)
1–12. Answers will vary.
13. Mayor Sandra A. Cummins
14. Mr. Peter Stone
15. Andrew Q. Jorgensen
16. Prof. Harlan; Dr. Watson; Thomas J. Bradley
17. Coach A. J. Brown
18. Seabiscuit
19. "Star Trek: The Next Generation,"; Mr. Data; Spot
20. Cinderella, Sleeping Beauty, Prince Charming

Capitalize and Italicize Titles (p. 39)
Answers will vary.

Capitalize With Quotation Marks (p. 40)
1. "Jingle Bells"
2. *Indiana Jones and the Temple of Doom*
3. *Cloudy With a Chance of Meatballs*
4. *The Boston Chronicle*
5. *Reader's Digest*
6. "101 Things You Can Do to Save Our Planet"
7. *The Merchant of Venice*
8. "The Emperor's New Clothes"
9. "Ode to the West Wind"
10. "Ask This Old House"

Capitalize Specific Locations (p. 41)
Answers will vary.

Capitalize Proper Nouns and Adjectives (p. 42)
1. Eun-Jung; Korean; English; Ukrainian
2. Chinese Checkers; Michigan Rummy
3. New York; Spanish; Italian; French; Canadian; Bermuda; Mexican; Greek
4. Swiss; Canadian; British Parliament; German; Polish
5. South America; Spanish
6. Brazil; Latin American; Portugal; Portuguese
7. Aunt Rachel; Persian; Arabian; Mexican
8. Egyptian; Hanging Gardens; Babylon
9. Elena; Norwegians; Swedes; Finns; Russians
10. Answers will vary.

What's on the Menu? (p. 43)
Denver omelet with Swiss cheese and Canadian bacon
New England clam chowder
Tex-Mex chili
meatballs on Italian bread
Polish sausage on German rye
Philly cheese steak
mashed Idaho potatoes with real lumps
French fries
Vidalia onion rings
Boston baked beans
Texas toast
Romaine lettuce salad with Russian dressing, Bermuda onions, and Roma tomatoes
Boston cream pie
French vanilla ice cream
Georgia peach pie
Colombian coffee
English tea
Florida orange juice

Places, Places (p. 44)
1. Minnesota; lakes
2. Neptune; Uranus; Mars; Venus; planets
3. Among; rivers; Earth; Amazon; Nile; Mississippi
4. Did; Earth; Milky Way Galaxy
5. Lake Titicaca; Peru; Bolivia
6. The; Christ; Mount Corcovado; Rio; Janeiro
7. Thomas Jefferson; Lewis; Clark; Pacific Ocean
8. Meriwether Lewis; William Clark; Missouri River; Great Falls

Addresses (p. 45)
1.	no	2.	yes	3.	yes
4.	yes	5.	no	6.	yes
7.	yes	8.	yes	9.	yes
10.	no	11.	no	12.	yes
13.	yes	14.	no	15.	yes

Abbreviations (p. 46)
1.	St.	2.	Ave.	3.	Blvd.
4.	NE	5.	Fr.	6.	Rev.
7.	Mt. St.	8.	Dr.	9.	Mrs.
10.	Atty.	11.	S.	12.	Sgt.
13.	Cr.	14.	MO	15.	Ln.

Special Days (p. 47)
All words listed should be capitalized except the words *of* and *the* in the holiday *Feast of the Three Kings,* the word *and* in *Aunt and Uncle Day,* the word *a* in *Tell a Joke Day,* and the word *of* in *International Day of Peace.*

Riddle Me (p. 48)
Capitalize the first word of each sentence and the words listed.
1. Iowa
2. New York; Mississippi River
3. Illinois; Missouri
4. New York City
5. Thanksgiving Day
6. Mount Everest
7. Friday; Thursday
8. January; Paris; France
9. (just first word *In*)
10. April; May; May
11. Santa; Christmas Eve
12. Wisconsin; Saturday
13. Texas; Rio Grande River
14. Tombstone, Arizona; Friday; Friday
15. Devonshire, England
16. Spain; Germany
17. New Mexico

Riddle Answers
1. Neither, they use a spoon.
2. Because he is still alive
3. Glass
4. Times Square
5. Be thankful you're not a turkey.
6. Mount Everest was still the tallest; it just hadn't been discovered yet.
7. In the dictionary
8. They were finished eating.
9. In February, because it's the shortest month
10. Pilgrims
11 Comet stayed home to clean the sink.
12. They go to the moo-vies.
13. Wet
14. His horse was named Friday.
15. Kittens
16. Neither, they both burn shorter.
17. The horses were too heavy to carry.

Acronyms (p. 49)
1. ASAP - as soon as possible
2. CIA - Central Intelligence Agency
3. COD - cash on delivery
4. GI - government issue
5. IRS - Internal Revenue Service
6. NBC - National Broadcasting Company
7. NFL - National Football League
8. PM - post meridian
9. PS - postscript
10. RN - registered nurse
11. RV - recreational vehicle
12. SCUBA - self-contained underwater breathing apparatus
13. UFO - unidentified flying object
14. VIP - very important person
15. BLT - bacon, lettuce, and tomato
16. FBI - Federal Bureau of Investigation
17. NASA - National Aeronautics and Space Administration

More Words to Capitalize (p. 50)
Answers will vary.

Odds and Ends (p. 51)
dear sid,

did you see the baseball history special on tv last night? my favorite story was the one about "shoeless" joe jackson. he began his baseball career as a pitcher but became an outfielder because his fast ball was so forceful it once broke a catcher's arm, and nobody would agree to catch for him.

you knew I was named for stan "the man" musial, the famous right fielder and first baseman for the st. louis cardinals, didn't you? my middle name, louis, came from the "iron horse," lou gehrig.

my dad played minor-league ball for a while and has always been a great baseball fan. he couldn't decide whether to name me ty, after the "georgia peach," ty cobb, or joe, after "joltin'" joe dimaggio. mom refused to consider the name george for george herman ruth because she thought a nickname like "babe" wouldn't be all that great when I grew up.

maybe this summer we can head up to the windy city and watch the cubbies play at wrigley field.

your cousin,
stan

Proofread the Trivia (p. 52)
1. People; Naples, Italy; Neopolitans
2. Some; Embarrass, MN; Square Butt, MT; Echo, TX
3. Did; Walt Disney; Donald Fauntleroy Duck
4. Some; TV; "Batman"; King Tut; Joker; Archer; Black Widow; Mad Hatter; Clock King

5. Adam West; Batman; Burt Ward; Robin; Boy Wonder
6. Andy Griffith; Sheriff Andy Taylor; Emmy; TV; "The Andy Griffith Show"; "Matlock"
7. Don Knotts; Deputy Barney Fife; Emmys
8. Before; Lassie; TV; *Lassie Come Home*; Eric Mowbray Knight
9. Caryn Johnson; Helena Rubenstein Children's Theatre; New York City
10. You; Caryn Johnson; Whoopi Goldberg

End Punctuation (p. 53)
1. Add question mark.
2. Add exclamation point.
3. Add period.
4. Add question mark.
5. Capitalize *Greek;* add period.
6. Add period.
7. Capitalize *Fill;* add period.
8. Add exclamation point after *Look* and after *already.*
9. Add question mark.
10. Add period.
11. Add exclamation point.
12. Capitalize *Giraffes*; add period.

Commas Separate (p. 54)
1. Thomas Jefferson, born on April 13, 1743, in Shadwell, Virginia, became the third president in March 1801.
2. Jefferson died on July 4, 1826, and was buried at his home near Charlottesville, Virginia.
3. Born in Hyde Park, New Jersey, in January 1882, Franklin D. Roosevelt died on April 12, 1945, shortly after he began his fourth term as president.
4. Three different men served as vice president with Franklin Roosevelt: John N. Garner, Henry A. Wallace, and Harry S Truman.
5. While president, Richard M. Nixon traveled to Moscow, Russia, and Beijing, China.
6. Theodore Roosevelt had six children: Alice, Theodore, Kermit, Ethel, Archibald, and Quentin.

Commas With Direct Address and Appositives (p. 55)
1. Barry,
2. Barry,
3. phobias, Barry
4. Santa Claus,
5. shy, Santa,
6. Boston, the city sometimes called Bean Town,
7. Calvin Coolidge, known as Silent Cal,
8. Harriet Tubman, nicknamed the "Moses of her people,"
9. Benjamin Franklin, the man who invented bifocals,
10. Acrophobia, the fear of heights, alektorophobia, the fear of chickens,

Commas With Independent Clauses (p. 56)
Answers may vary. Possible answers given.
1. Abby raked the leaves into piles, and Andy put the leaves into bags.
2. Beth wanted to spend the day at the mall, but she also wanted to spend the day at the beach.
3. Carlos fixed my bicycle, but he could not fix my car.
4. Diane ate three helpings of spaghetti for supper, but she was too full for dessert.
5. Ethan ran a good race, but Ellen finished in first place.
6. Chuck washed the windows of his '57 Chevy, and he checked the oil, but he forgot to fill it with gas.

A Few More Ways to Use Commas (p. 57)
1. cooked,
2. barbecued,
3. ate,
4. bakes,
5. No,
6. vacuum,
7. Santa,
8. truly,
9. left,
10. stopped,

Quotations (p. 58)
1. After serving one term as president, Calvin Coolidge stated, "I do not choose to run for President in 1928."
2. When asked why, Coolidge replied, "Because there's no chance for advancement."
3. "There, I guess King George will be able to read that," stated John Hancock after he signed his name in large letters on the Declaration of Independence.
4. "People who are wrapped up in themselves make small packages," wrote Benjamin Franklin.
5. "Now that I realize what they've had to put up with," wrote Betty Ford about being the first lady, "I have a new respect and admiration for every one of them."

Yogi-isms (p. 59)
1. "A nickel ain't worth a dime anymore," he complained.
2. "It's never happened in World Series history, and it hasn't happened since," Yogi told fans.
3. "It's déjà vu all over again!" he exclaimed.
4. Yogi advised, "When you come to a fork in the road, take it."
5. He also said, "We're lost, but we're making good time."
6. "If I didn't wake up, I'd still be sleeping," he said.
7. Some of Yogi's advice was confusing, like the time he said, "Always go to other people's funerals; otherwise, they won't go to yours."
8. "Little League baseball is a good thing 'cause it keeps the parents off the streets, and it keeps the kids out of the house!" he told a reporter.
9. "The future ain't what it used to be," Yogi said, and I think he was right.
10. Yogi once said, "I never said most of the things I said."

11. "You've got to be very careful if you don't know where you are going, because you might not get there." was one of Yogi's quotes that left people scratching their heads.
12. "Pair up in threes," he told the players.
13. Yogi said, "I usually take a two-hour nap from one to four," so it was hard to know when he would be awake.
14. "We made too many wrong mistakes," Yogi explained.
15. Try to remember that Yogi advised, "If the world were perfect, it wouldn't be."

Proofreading (p. 60)
Group 1
A. Delete comma after *Jake*.
B. Correct
C. Replace period with question mark at end of sentence.
D. Add comma after *glasses*.
Group 2
A. Correct
B. Add quotation marks around "Let me out,"
C. Add comma after *flared*.
D. Replace question mark with period at end of sentence.
Group 3
A. Add comma after *thunder*.
B. Add comma after *bed*.
C. Add comma after *bed, dresser, posters, stinky*.
D. Correct

Contractions (p. 61)
2. they're
3. she's
4. we've, they've
5. you'd, she'd, they'd
6. I'll, you'll, we'll, she'll, he'll, they'll
7. didn't
8. shouldn't
9. hadn't
10. won't
11. would + not
12. could + not
13. have + not
14. shall + not
15. can + not

Write the Contractions (p. 62)
1. aren't
2. I've
3. He's
4. won't
5. would've
6. she'll
7. doesn't
8. Don't
9. You'd
10. they're
11. shouldn't
12. What's; It's

Apostrophes With Singular Possessives (p. 63)
1. the man's monkeys
2. Oscar's orange octopus
3. Dr. Seuss's stories
4. a child's grandparents
5. Agnes's aches
6. a fly's wings
7. a zebra's stripes
8. Pat's pajamas
9. a mouse's houses
10. a goose's eggs

Apostrophes With Plural Possessives (p. 64)
1. the geese's eggs
2. the woman's clubs
3. the women's club
4. the birds' nests
5. the grandparents' grandchildren
6. the fly's eyes
7. the flies' eyes
8. the mice's houses

Possessive Pronouns (p. 65)
1. hers
2. her
3. mine
4. my
5. yours
6. your
7. its
8. his
9. their
10. theirs

Contractions and Possessive Pronouns (p. 66)
1. It's; its
2. You're; your
3. They're; their
4. theirs; there's
5. It's
6. your
7. There's
8. its
9. you're
10. their
11. theirs
12. there's

Introducing: The Colon (p. 67)
1. reason:
2. Hawaii:
3. saw:
4. enjoyed:
5. together:
6. no colon needed
7. no colon needed
8. state:
9. states:
10. time:

Five More Ways to Use a Colon (p. 68)
1. 11:55
2. Proverbs 24:26
3. *Seabiscuit: An American Legend*
4. Dear Mr. President:
5. (*Twelfth Night* II:5)
6. Answers will vary.

Semicolons (p. 69)
1. sheep,
2. alone;
3. lamb;
4. clock, and
5. laughed;
6. meadow,
7. nimble;
8. hill,
9. cockleshells,
10. shoe,

Dashes and Semicolons (p. 70)
1. I'll pick you up at 7:30—no, make it 7:10—and we'll go rock climbing.
2. The pilot flew to Rome, Italy; Frankfurt, Germany; Paris, France; and London, England, last week.
3. Let's follow the west trail—or would you rather not?
4. All the people from the village—men, women, children—joined the animals fleeing the out-of-control fire.
5. Lincoln was a tall man who wore a top hat—a most unusual sight to be sure.
6. I'd like a chocolate shake—better make that a diet soda. I'm trying to lose weight.
7. Dear Library Director:
8. Would you please order more historical fiction like *The Black Flower: A Novel of the Civil War* for our library?

Punctuation Review (p. 71)
Answers will vary.